Report on the Youth Labor Force

U.S. Department of Labor
Alexis M. Herman, Secretary

June 2000

Revised, November 2000

Preface

I remember my first job—I worked as a summer camp counselor and taught young campers how to tap dance. It was a lot of fun. I worked most summers in my teen years and through college. I still use what I learned from those jobs every day as Secretary of Labor. I truly value those experiences and I'm an avid supporter of jobs for young workers.

I know that parents also understand how important early work experiences are. They know intuitively what this report suggests—that teenagers who deliver newspapers, bag groceries, or serve hamburgers in their after-school jobs are often more likely to go to college and have better lifelong careers. And make more money, too.

Employers, parents, schools, and government must continue to support positive work experiences for our youngest workers—but with two critical caveats: they must be safe work experiences and work should never interfere with school.

We must be especially diligent in ensuring that our most vulnerable young workers, the children of migrant farm workers, are protected through strict enforcement of child labor laws in the fields. And they must be given every opportunity to get a good education.

I welcome this report. It provides the information we need to make wise policy decisions. Protecting our youngest workers is vital to our national interest. They should have the opportunity to experience the rewards and dignity of work without jeopardizing their education, their health, or their lives.

ALEXIS M. HERMAN, Secretary
U.S. Department of Labor

Acknowledgments

This *Report on the Youth Labor Force* provides a detailed, overall look at youth labor in the United States, including regulations on child labor, current work experience of youths and how it has changed over time, and the outcomes of this experience. It draws on a variety of Department of Labor data sources in developing this picture.

The report was prepared under the overall direction of Marilyn Manser, an associate commissioner with the Bureau of Labor Statistics (BLS), who also was responsible for the introduction. The second chapter describes the history of child labor in the United States, and details the current Federal and State regulations covering child labor. It was written by Art Kerschner, Jr., leader, Child Labor and Special Employment Team, with the Labor Department's Employment Standards Administration. The third chapter, contributed by Donna Rothstein, a research economist at BLS, and Diane Herz, an economist also at BLS, provides a detailed current look at the work experiences of youth aged 15 and under. The fourth chapter examines the current employment and unemployment status of youths aged 15 to 17, and looks at how this youth employment and unemployment has changed over the past 20 years. It was pre-

pared by Diane Herz and Karen Kosanovich, also an economist with BLS. The appendix to chapter 4, which compares results from the National Longitudinal Survey of Youth and the Current Population Survey, was written by Donna Rothstein and Diane Herz. The fifth chapter takes a separate look at youth employment in agriculture, a sector in which young workers have characteristics that are, on average, different from those of their counterparts in other industries and face different regulations. It was prepared by Ruth Samardick, survey statistician with the Labor Department's Assistant Secretary for Policy; Susan M. Gabbard, a senior associate with Aguirre International; and Melissa A. Lewis, a research associate also with Aguirre International. The sixth chapter, written by Anthony Barkume, research economist with BLS, addresses the health and safety of young workers. The final chapter, contributed by Donna Rothstein and Marilyn Manser, provides data on the relationship between work intensity at ages 16 and 17 and later college attendance and the amount of work experience from age 18 through 30. It also reviews the extensive research literature on the effect of working while young on later educational and labor market outcomes.

Contents

Chapter 1.
Introduction

Issues involving child labor are important throughout the world. Laws and regulations limiting the extent and type of work that children can perform have been in place in the United States for many years. These regulations reflect society's concern about preserving children's safety and well-being and ensuring that children have sufficient time available for their schooling. Within the constraints of these regulations, youths engage in a significant amount of work activity, both in informal jobs, such as mowing lawns and babysitting, and in regular "employee" jobs.

A brief summary of key aspects of the U.S. laws and regulations governing child labor is presented in exhibit 1.1. Given these regulations, child labor in the United States generally means labor by teenagers. Regulations differ by age of the youth, with tighter restrictions for those aged 14 to 15 than for those aged 16 to 17. Rules also differ between the agricultural and nonagricultural sectors of the economy.

This report has three main purposes. First, it explains the current U.S. regulations governing child labor. Second, it provides a detailed look at youth labor in this country, including how it differs among major demographic groups, between the agricultural and nonagricultural sectors, and over time. Third, it describes the outcomes of young people's work activities, including occupational injuries and fatalities and other, longer-term

This chapter was contributed by Marilyn Manser, an associate commissioner with the Bureau of Labor Statistics.

consequences. Much government information is published regularly for the standard classification of 16- to 19-year-olds. This report contributes to knowledge by presenting information not normally provided for youths under 18 years of age. Exhibit 1.2 shows the datasets that form the basis for the analysis presented in later chapters. Although data availability places some constraints on the information that can be provided for youths of different ages, these sources permit us to present a rich picture of youth labor in the United States.

How did regulations on child labor evolve in this country, and what is their current status? Chapter 2 of this report addresses these questions, looking at both Federal and State laws and regulations and current policy approaches.

What is the current situation regarding the employment of youths? Chapters 3 and 4 present detailed information on this topic. The vast majority of American youths engage in some labor market activities while enrolled in school. Using data from the National Longitudinal Survey of Youth 1997 (NLSY97), the authors of chapter 3 demonstrate that work activity is substantial even among 14- and 15-year-olds. Chapter 4 presents data on employment and unemployment of 15- to 17-year-olds from the Current Population Survey (CPS). It shows that, while it is not commonly recognized, the percentage of teens aged 15 to 17 who are employed actually has fallen somewhat over the past 20 years. (NOTE: In these chapters, we also will discuss what has hap-

pened to the actual levels of teen employment.) Although both chapters 3 and 4 discuss employment of youths in all industries, we break out agriculture for separate attention in chapter 5 because it has special characteristics, and is subject to different regulations regarding child labor than are nonagricultural industries. In all three of these chapters on youth employment, we detail substantial differences among demographic groups in the probability that a youth works and in the amount and types of work performed.

Youths benefit from pay received for this work, but do these work experiences provide other benefits or costs? To address this question, chapter 6 examines youth safety in the workplace. Job-related youth fatalities, which varied between 62 and 70 per year over the period 1992–97, disproportionately occurred in family businesses and in agriculture. The incidence of lost worktime injuries among youths fell over this same period. Youth employment may have long-term consequences, including effects on educational attainment and future employment and wage growth. Chapter 7 presents information from the NLSY79 on college attendance and labor market experience of persons while they were aged 18 to 30, examined separately for individuals categorized by work activity while aged 16 to 17. The generally positive relationship shown does not necessarily imply cause and effect. Chapter 7 also briefly discusses the considerable literature that has emerged from attempts to identify the educational and labor market outcomes of early work experience.

Exhibit 1.1. Federal limits on the hours that youths may work and the types of work that they may perform in nonagricultural industries[1]

Age of youth	Limits on the type of work	Limits on number of hours and time of the day
16- to 17-year-olds	Banned from performing those occupations that the Secretary of Labor determines to be particularly hazardous for this age group.	No limits.
14- to 15-year-olds	Banned from work in most industries and from various occupations. May be employed in retail, food service, and gasoline service establishments.	There are limits on the total number of hours per day and per week, as well as on the time of day, that work may be performed.
Under 14 years of age	Banned from most work. May perform tasks for which no covered employment relationship arises, such as babysitting on a part-time, irregular basis.	

[1] For the nonagricultural sector, there are exceptions to these rules. Rules differ for agricultural work. See ch. 2 for details.

Exhibit 1.2. Datasets used in this report

Dataset	Coverage	Periodicity	Type of information	Other
National Longitudinal Survey of Youth 1979 (NLSY79)	Cohort of individuals aged 14 to 22 in 1979	Annual through 1994; biennial 1996-present	Longitudinal survey. Extensive information on work experience, education, and a variety of social and demographic factors.	Interviews with youth respondents
National Longitudinal Survey of Youth 1997 (NLSY97)	Cohort of individuals aged 12 to 17 in 1997	Annual	Longitudinal survey. Round 1, collected in 1997, contains extensive information on youth work experience, education, family background, and a variety of other social and demographic factors.	Interviews with youth respondents
Current Population Survey (CPS)	Individuals aged 15 and older in households	Monthly	Primarily cross-sectional. (Also provides short-term longitudinal information on individuals, who are interviewed 8 times in 16 months.) Focus on current labor force behavior. Contains demographic information.	Accepts proxy respondents
National Agricultural Workers Survey (NAWS)	Farmworkers performing crop agriculture	Annual	Cross-sectional survey. Information on demographics, migration, well-being.	Interviews with respondents aged 14 and older. Also obtains information on children of farmworkers.
Census of Fatal Occupational Injuries (CFOI)	All industries	Annual	Census. Information on type of injury, worker demographics.	Information obtained from multiple sources
Survey of Occupational Injuries and Illnesses (SOII)	Establishments in private industry (except private households and employers with 10 or fewer employees in agriculture)	Annual	Information on types of cases and basic worker demographics.	

Chapter 2.
Child Labor Laws and Enforcement

Introduction

This chapter looks briefly at the history of child labor in the United States, and discusses how that history influences youth employment today. It then examines the current Federal child labor provisions, provides a comparison of State child labor laws, and discusses other government programs that directly affect the employment of young workers. The chapter concludes with a discussion of the U.S. Department of Labor's strategy for combating oppressive child labor and the effectiveness of its compliance strategy.

History of child labor in the United States

Children have worked in America, contributing to the well-being of the family unit, since the arrival of the first colonists. European settlers, bringing social values with them that equated idleness with pauperism, were quick to pass laws that actually required children to work. For example, in 1641, the court of Massachusetts Bay ordered all households to work on wild hemp for clothing, and it was expected that "children should be industriously implied (sic)."[1] Adopting "poor laws" similar to the English laws, the colonies required the apprenticeship of poor children—some at ages as young as 3 years. Children worked on family farms and in family cottage industries. The institution of slavery also encompassed the labor of children born or sold into servitude.

The industrial revolution ushered in the modern factory system and changed a predominately rural populace into an urban one. Factory towns grew up dependent on a labor supply of women and children, the children working not necessarily as apprentices but as factory labor. Children were seen as a cheap and manageable source of labor. Newspaper advertisements of the day reflected the fact that factory managers preferred to hire families with several children, and widows with children were especially favored.

Child labor in this country was so widespread, and so much a part of economic reality in the early part of the 19th century, that no one looked toward or expected its abolition. But as the number of factories multiplied and the child workforce grew, the social conscience began to stir—not against child labor itself, but against some features of the factory system as they affected the children.

The earliest concerns were that factory children were growing up without receiving even a modest education. Long workdays and workweeks left little time for study. In 1813, Connecticut enacted a law encouraging manufacturers to provide young employees with lessons in reading, writing, and arithmetic, but the law was ineffective. It was not until 1836 that Massachusetts passed this country's first child labor law—legislation that required children under the age of 15 employed in manufacturing to spend at least 3 months each year in school. A few States soon adopted similar laws.

After the Civil War, industry expanded and became increasingly mechanized. The textile industry flourished in the South and with it, oppressive child labor. Children as young as 6 or 7 years were recruited to work 13-hour days, for miniscule wages, in hot and dusty factories. Proposals to change these conditions met with stiff opposition. By the turn of the century, only a few southern States had passed laws limiting the number of hours that children could work.

The early 1900s saw a growing acceptance of the concept that States should provide for the general protection of children. In 1909, the Bureau of Labor Statistics issued a landmark report on working women and children. This 19-volume report confirmed that more children were employed in the South than in New England. The report also found that, in a substantial number of cases, children's earnings were essential to meeting their families' needs, but that in other cases, families would not have suffered financial hardships if child labor were forbidden.[2]

By 1913, all but nine States had fixed 14 years as the minimum age for factory work, and a majority of the States had extended this minimum to stores and other specified places of employment.[3] Although Congress had made several attempts to restrict oppressive child labor, the attempts had failed, usually on constitutional grounds. It was not until 1938, with the passage of the Fair Labor Standards Act (upheld by the Supreme Court in 1941) that meaningful Federal child labor legislation was enacted. The Fair Labor Standards Act (FLSA) remains the Federal law governing minimum wages, overtime, child labor, and recordkeeping. The child labor provisions of the FLSA establish a minimum age of 16 years for covered nonagricultural employment. However, they allow 14- and 15-year-olds to be employed in occupations other than in mining and manufacturing if the Secretary of Labor determines that the employment is confined to periods that will not interfere with their schooling and to conditions that will not interfere with their health and well-being. The FLSA also prohibits minors under age 18 from working in occupations that the Secretary of Labor declares to be particularly hazardous for such youths or detrimental to their health or well-being.

The nature of child labor in the United States has changed over the last 50 years. Child labor now means, almost exclusively, teenagers—teenagers who are generally full-time students and part-time employees. But even with the increased emphasis on education and the improved economic conditions that this century has brought, the Nation's young people are still working today, and in large numbers.

The unique history of the United States, which both fostered and overcame some of the most oppressive types of child labor, still helps to create an environment conducive to youth employment that differs considerably from that of other industrialized nations. The most often cited difference is that the proportion of teens who work is relatively high in the United States compared with other developed countries.[4] Americans have always tenaciously believed in the value of work, for themselves and for their children. They believe that positive work experiences during the teenage years can benefit a person's development, maturity, and sense of responsibility. Conversely, idleness is associated with delinquency.

Another difference lies in the reasons why teenagers, who have not yet completed their formal educations, seek employment. For the most part, the jobs held by U.S. teens are not conceived as stepping-stones on a life career path. Other developed countries, such as Germany, Denmark, and Switzerland, have long included adolescent employment as part of formal apprenticeship, School-to-Work, and Work Experience and Career Exploration Programs that are closely linked to the educational process and lead to specific adult jobs. Only in the last two decades has there been a concerted effort in the United States to link adolescent work experiences with school curricula to facilitate the transition from student to worker. The little research that has been done on why U.S. teens seek paying jobs suggests that the primary reason is money, not the value of the work experience.[5] E. Greenberger and G. Steinberg reported in 1986 that 74 percent of employed high school students in their sample said money was the primary reason for having a job.[6] Most working teens spend their earnings as discretionary income, rather than helping to meet family expenses. And the size and impact of that discretionary income is enormous.

The Nation's roots also affect the types of jobs legally available to young workers. The United States began as a nation of farmers, and agriculture continues to enjoy a special place in the perceptions of its citizens. Growing up on the family farm, learning the value of hard work in the fresh air, is still viewed by many as the perfect childhood. Federal and State child labor laws governing agricultural employment reflect this belief—they are much less restrictive than those applied to other industries.[7] Children working on farms owned or operated by a parent are completely exempt from Federal agricultural child labor provisions, and other teenage farmworkers are permitted to perform hazardous jobs at younger ages than are their counterparts who work in other industries.

International child labor

Although this report concentrates on child labor in the United States, it is both important and appropriate to mention the circumstances of child workers in other countries. The dichotomy that exists between industrialized countries and developing countries is especially apparent when one looks at child labor. As previously noted, child labor in industrialized countries almost exclusively means adolescents who are full-time students with part-time jobs. But child labor often wears a much different face in developing countries.

The International Labor Organization (ILO) estimates that more than 250 million children are working around the world, often in occupations that are "detrimental to their physical, mental and emotional well-being."[8] An estimated 120 million children work full time, with no opportunities for education and the accompanying promise of a better future. These youths have been found working as miners; as laborers in rug, textile, glass, and brick manufacturing establishments; as domestic servants; and as prostitutes.

But there is cause for hope. Over the past few years, child labor has grabbed the attention of the international community, provoking worldwide discussion of this issue. Numerous international organizations, governments in both developing and industrialized countries, and advocacy groups are creating and implementing strategies and initiatives to address child labor.

The United States has taken the lead on a number of fronts. The Department of Labor's Bureau of International Labor Affairs has studied and reported on international child labor in its *By the Sweat and Toil of Children* series. The United States also is supporting direct action to improve the lives of working children around the world by committing $37.1 million to fund activities that address international child labor, including nearly $30 million in Fiscal Year 1999 to support the ILO's International Program on the Elimination of Child Labor (ILO-IPEC). IPEC initiatives strive to take children out of the workplace and place them in the classroom without jeopardizing family units and incomes.

Federal child labor laws

As mentioned earlier, the Fair Labor

Standards Act of 1938 (FLSA) is the framework for Federal child labor provisions. The Wage and Hour Division of the U.S. Department of Labor's Employment Standards Administration is charged with the enforcement of the FLSA.

To be subject to the provisions of the FLSA, an employee must be employed by a covered enterprise[9] or individually engaged in interstate commerce or in the production of goods for interstate commerce, or in any closely related process or occupation directly essential to such production. Not all employment of young workers is covered under the FLSA. In addition, some jobs held by youths, such as delivering newspapers and performing in motion pictures and theatrical, radio, and television productions, are specifically exempted from the child labor provisions of the FLSA.

Nonagricultural employment. Under the FLSA, 16 is the minimum age for nonagricultural employment, but 14- and 15-year-olds may be employed for certain periods—which do not interfere with their schooling—in jobs that the Secretary of Labor has determined will not interfere with their health and well-being. Children under 14 years of age are generally too young for formal employment unless they meet a specific exemption.[10] However, these youths may perform tasks where no covered employment relationship arises—such as babysitting on a part-time, irregular basis or performing minor chores around private homes. The Secretary has promulgated child labor provisions governing the employment of 14- and 15-year-olds; these are found in Subpart C of Regulations, 29 CFR Part 570 (Child Labor Reg. 3). Exhibit 2.1 displays the Federal child labor provisions governing the nonagricultural employment of 14- and 15-year-olds. There are some exceptions to these provisions for students enrolled in a State Work Experience and Career Exploration Program (WECEP) that have been authorized by the U. S. Department of Labor. The special child labor provisions governing the em-

ployment of WECEP participants are listed in exhibit 2.2.

Teenagers 16 years of age and older may work at any time of the day and for unlimited hours. The FLSA prohibits workers under 18 years of age from performing those nonagricultural occupations that the Secretary of Labor declares to be particularly hazardous for the employment of children under 18 years of age or detrimental to their health or well-being. There are currently 17 Hazardous Occupations Orders (HOs), which are contained in Subpart E of Regulations, 29 CFR Part 570 (Occupations Particularly Hazardous for the Employment of Minors Between 16 and 18 Years of Age or Detrimental to Their Health or Well-Being). Exhibit 2.3 displays the industries and occupations covered by the current Hazardous Occupations Orders. Certain of the HOs contain limited exemptions that permit bonafide apprentices and student learners to perform otherwise prohibited work as part of their on-the-job training.

Agricultural employment. Unlike the rules governing nonagricultural employment, most of the child labor provisions applicable to agricultural employment are statutory. Under Federal law:

- A child working in agriculture on a farm owned or operated by his or her parent is exempted from Federal agricultural child labor provisions.

- Young farmworkers who are not the children of the farmer employing them are subject to Federal child labor provisions that differ by age:

  - Youths are no longer subject to the Federal agricultural child labor provisions when they reach 16 years of age.

  - Children aged 14 or 15 may perform any nonhazardous farm job outside of school hours, and, with proper training and certifi-

cation, they also may perform certain hazardous duties.

- Children aged 12 or 13 may be employed outside of school hours in nonhazardous jobs, but only on the farm on which their parent works or with the written consent of a parent.

- Children under 12 may be employed outside of school hours in nonhazardous jobs on farms *not* subject to the Fair Labor Standards Act (FLSA) minimum wage[11] if their parent also is employed on that farm, or with parental consent.

- Children aged 10 or 11 may be employed to hand-harvest short-season crops outside of school hours under special waivers granted by the U.S. Department of Labor.[12]

As directed by the FLSA, the Secretary of Labor has found and declared certain agricultural tasks to be particularly hazardous for employees below the age of 16. The Agriculture Hazardous Occupations Orders (HO/As), listed in exhibit 2.4, are contained in section 570.71 of Regulations, 29 CFR Part 570. As noted, farmworkers as young as 14 years of age may perform some tasks otherwise prohibited by the Agricultural Hazardous Occupations Orders after completing, and in some cases participating in, certain vocational training programs. The FLSA prohibits hired farmworkers under 16 years of age from working during school hours, but does not give the Secretary of Labor authority to prohibit their employment during other times of the day or limit the number of daily or weekly hours they may be employed.

Other child labor standards

There are other labor standards laws, both State and Federal, that regulate the hours of work, types of jobs, and working conditions of children and adolescents.

Exhibit 2.1.

Federal Limits on the Hours and the Type of Work
That 14- and 15-Year-Olds May Perform[1]

Youths 14 and 15 years of age may be employed outside school hours in a variety of nonmanufacturing and nonhazardous jobs under specified conditions. There are limits on both the duties these youths may perform and the hours they may work.

Occupation restrictions

Banned from performing most work but may be employed in retail, food service, and gasoline service establishments.

Banned from working in manufacturing, processing, or mining, or in any workroom or workplace in which goods are manufactured, processed, or mined.

Banned from performing any work the Secretary has declared to be hazardous for young workers by issuing Hazardous Occupations Orders (HOs).

Banned from occupations involving transportation, construction, warehousing, or communication, or occupations involving the use of power-driven machinery.

May perform some cooking at snack bars and in fast-food places in full sight of customers, but banned from performing baking.

Hours restrictions

The Regulations limit the hours and times of day during which 14- and 15-year-olds may work to:

- outside school hours;
- not more than 40 hours in any one week when school is not in session;
- not more than 18 hours in any one week when school is in session;
- not more than 8 hours in any day when school is not in session;
- not more than 3 hours in any day when school is in session; and
- between 7 a.m. and 7 p.m., except during the summer (June 1 through Labor Day), when the evening work limit is 9 p.m.

---

[1] Limited exceptions to the hours and occupations standards are permissible for students participating in bona fide Work Experience and Career Exploration Programs. See exhibit 2.2.

Exhibit 2.2.

Work Experience and Career Exploration Programs (WECEP) Federal Limits on the Hours and the Type of Work That Participants May Perform

The WECEP is designed to provide a carefully planned work experience and career exploration program for 14- and 15-year-old youths, including students enrolled in School-to-Work curricula, who can benefit from a career-oriented educational program. The WECEP is especially conducive to helping youths to become reoriented and motivated toward education, and to prepare for the world of work.

Occupation restrictions

WECEP participants are subject to the same child labor rules governing the employment of all 14- and 15-year-olds, but the WECEP regulations do allow participants to be employed in certain occupations otherwise prohibited for minors in this age group, after receiving a variance from the Administrator of the U.S. Department of Labor's Wage and Hour Division.

Hours restrictions

The WECEP Regulations permit participants to work more hours and at different times than other 14- and 15-year olds. WECEP participants may work:

- during school hours;
- not more than 40 hours in any one week when school is not in session;
- not more than 23 hours in any one week when school is in session;
- not more than 8 hours in any day when school is not in session;
- not more than 3 hours in any day when school is in session; and
- between 7 a.m. and 7 p.m., except during the summer (June 1 through Labor Day), when the evening hour is 9 p.m.

The rules governing WECEPs are found in §570.35a of Regulations, 29 CFR Part 570. Approval to operate a WECEP is granted to State departments of education by the Administrator of the Wage and Hour Division for a 2-year period. In order to participate, youths must be 14 or 15 years of age and be identified by their teachers, counselors, or other school officials as being able to benefit from the program.

Exhibit 2.3.

The Hazardous Occupations Orders
Federal Ban on the Work Activities of
16- and 17-Year-Olds in Nonagricultural Employment

The Fair Labor Standards Act establishes an 18-year minimum age for those occupations that the Secretary of Labor finds and declares to be particularly hazardous for 16- and 17-year-old minors, or detrimental to their health or well-being. The rules for the Hazardous Occupations Orders (HOs) are provided for in Subpart E of Regulations, 29 CFR Part 570 (§§570.50 through 570.68). There are currently 17 HOs, which include a partial or total ban on the following:[1]

Working with explosives and radioactive materials;

Operating motor vehicles or working as outside helpers on motor vehicles (except in very limited circumstances);

Mining activities, including coal mining; metal mining; and other mining, including sand and gravel operations;

Operating most power-driven woodworking, and certain metalworking, machines;

Operating power-driven bakery, meat processing, and paper products machinery, including meat slicers and most paper balers and compactors;

Operating various types of power-driven saws and guillotine shears;

Operating most power-driven hoisting apparatus, such as nonautomatic elevators, forklifts, and cranes;

Most jobs in slaughtering and meatpacking establishments;

Most jobs in excavation, logging, saw-milling, roofing, wrecking, demolition, and ship-breaking; and

Most jobs in the manufacturing of bricks, tiles, and similar products.

---

[1] §570.50 provides a limited exemption from certain of the HOs for bona fide apprentices and student-learners who are at least 16 years of age.

Exhibit 2.4.

The Hazardous Occupations Orders in Agriculture
Federal Ban on Work Activities of Minors Under Age 16
in Agricultural Work

The Fair Labor Standards Act establishes a 16-year minimum age for those occupations in agriculture that the Secretary of Labor finds and declares to be particularly hazardous. The Hazardous Occupations Orders in Agriculture (HO/A) are contained in §570.71 of Subpart E-1 of Regulations, 29 CFR Part 570, and ban the following work activities in agricultural employment:[1]

Operating a tractor of over 20 horsepower, or connecting or disconnecting an implement or any of its parts to or from such a tractor;

Operating or assisting to operate any of the following machines:[1] corn picker, cotton picker, grain combine, hay mower, forage harvester, hay baler, potato digger, mobile pea viner, feed grinder, crop dryer, forage blower, auger conveyor, the unloading mechanism of a gravity-type self-unloading wagon or trailer, trencher, forklift, potato combine, power post-hole digger, power post driver, nonwalking type rotary tiller, and power-driven circular, band, or chain saws;

Working on a farm in a yard, pen, or stall occupied by a bull, boar, or stud horse maintained for breeding purposes; or a sow with suckling pigs; or a cow with newborn calf;

Felling, buckling, skidding, loading, or unloading timber with a butt diameter of more than 6 inches;

Working from a ladder or scaffold at a height of over 20 feet;

Driving a bus, truck, or automobile when transporting passengers, or riding on a tractor as a passenger or helper;

Working inside a fruit, forage, or grain storage designed to retain an oxygen-deficient or toxic atmosphere; in an upright silo within 2 weeks after silage has been added or when a top unloading device is in operating position; in a manure pit; or in a horizontal silo while operating a tractor for packing purposes;

Handling (including performing certain related duties) or applying pesticides and other agricultural chemicals classified as Category I or II of toxicity by the Federal Insecticide, Fungicide, and Rodenticide Act;

Handling or using a blasting agent, including dynamite, black powder, sensitized ammonium nitrate, blasting caps, and primer cord; or

Transporting, transferring, or applying anhydrous ammonia.

---

[1] §570.52 permits certain vocational agricultural student-learners and those who have successfully completed approved training courses to perform certain tasks otherwise prohibited by the Agricultural Hazardous Occupations Orders when they are 14 years of age.

State child labor laws. The adoption of compulsory school attendance laws by the States has done much to curb oppressive child labor in America. Every State also has a child labor law, usually enforced by a State labor department, that strives to preserve the health, education, and well-being of young workers. These laws, which often share extensive overlap in coverage with the FLSA, vary in the level of protection afforded young workers for both agricultural and nonagricultural employment. Within any State law, there may be some provisions that are more or less restrictive than provisions of the Federal law. If both the State and Federal law apply to the same employment situation, the more stringent standard of the two must be obeyed. The level of enforcement of State laws also varies widely.

While the laws differ from State to State in the standards prescribed, in the range of occupations covered, and in the age brackets to which they apply, Federal law is generally more stringent than the State laws with respect to prohibiting work in occupations involving physical hazards and assessing penalties for violations. This is true for both agricultural and nonagricultural employment. Federal law also is the same or more restrictive with respect to the minimum age for general employment. On the other hand, many State laws mandate standards that are absent from Federal law, such as maximum hours and night work restrictions for 16- and 17-year-olds, prohibitions on employment in occupations or in places detrimental to morals (hotel and liquor service), and mandatory work permits or age certificates.

Unlike the FLSA, more than half of the States regulate the daily or weekly number of hours that 16- and 17-year-olds may be employed, or restrict the evening hours during which 16- and 17-year-olds may work, or both. State hours and time-of-work regulations on the whole, however, tend to be less restrictive for minors under the age of 16 than are the Federal regulations. Many States do not

further limit the number of hours that youths under 16 years of age can work during a school day or week while school is in session. Of those that do limit work during the school year, many permit longer hours of work than allowed by the FLSA. Still other States allow teenagers to work later in the evening than permitted by Federal rules.

Seventeen States (primarily in the South) either exempt agricultural employment entirely or do not identify it as a covered industry under the State's child labor laws.[13] Eight States place restrictions on agricultural employment similar to Federal standards.[14] Eight States have restricted daily or weekly hours of work, or both, for minors under the age of 18 employed in agriculture.[15] Twelve States impose a higher age standard than do the Federal provisions and prohibit 16- and 17-year-olds from working in certain hazardous occupations; some restrictions may apply to agriculture.[16] In some cases, States have specifically adopted standards for agriculture that are more stringent than those of the Federal government. For example, Florida prohibits youths under age of 18 from operating or assisting in the operation of tractors over 20 PTO (power take-off) horsepower, earth-moving equipment, and other related machinery. Oregon precludes anyone under 18 years of age from operating power-driven farm equipment of any kind. A more detailed discussion and comparison of State and Federal child labor provisions, for both agricultural and nonagricultural employment, can be found on the U.S. Department of Labor's Website at **http://www.dol.gov/dol/esa/public/programs/whd/state/state.htm**.

Though not conceived as labor standards legislation, State laws that establish minimum ages and other criteria for operating motor vehicles on public roads also affect youth employment and the types of jobs available to teens. These rules apply equally to on-the-job driving and to personal, non-employment situations. Automobile crashes have remained a leading cause of teen occupational and nonoccupa-

tional deaths since the 1980s.[17] Many States have adopted systems of "graduated licensing" as a strategy to reduce automobile crashes involving teens.[18] Graduated licensing is a system that phases young beginners into full driving privileges as they mature and demonstrate that they have acquired driving skills.

Occupational Safety and Health Administration and Worker's Compensation Provisions. The Occupational Safety and Health Act (29 U.S.C. Chapter 15, Section 651 et seq.), enacted in 1970, requires that employers provide work and places of employment that comply with specific safety and health standards and that are free from other recognized hazards that may cause serious physical harm. Working children and adolescents are entitled to the same protections as adults but, in most cases, receive no additional protection.[19] The Occupational Safety and Health Act, administered by the Occupational Safety and Health Administration (OSHA), requires that State regulations be as protective as the Federal rules. Some States have adopted rules that are more protective than the Federal rules. Most Federal and State occupational safety and health rules do not apply to agricultural employment.

State workers' compensation programs also affect the health and safety of working youths. Many programs provide, or have the potential to provide, incentives for employers to improve working conditions for all employees. State workers' compensation agencies also provide a range of services to help employers identify and correct real or potential workplace hazards.

Current strategy for ensuring compliance

Protecting the health and safety of young workers, while helping them enjoy positive work experiences, remains a high priority of the U.S. Department of Labor. Consistent with her goal of assuring every U.S. worker—and especially young workers—a safe, healthful, and fair workplace, Secretary of Labor Alexis Herman launched the Department's *Safe Work/ Safe Kids* initiative last June. *Safe Work/Safe Kids* is designed to focus public attention on the issues of child labor and both educate and mobilize all those who can positively affect youth employment.

In order to help teens have safe and constructive early work experiences, *Safe Work/Safe Kids* employs a comprehensive strategy of enhanced, targeted *enforcement*; increased compliance *education and outreach*; construction of strong *partnerships;* and creation of heightened *public awareness*. These four components, employed simultaneously, greatly magnify the positive compliance effects that would be obtained if any were employed independent of the others. Effective, credible, and targeted enforcement, which serves to detect, remedy, penalize, and deter violations, is a key component of the compliance strategy. Industries targeted for enforcement initiatives in 1999 included agriculture, through the "*Salad Bowl*" initiative; retail trade, especially restaurants; garment manufacturing; and health care. The use of the "hot goods" provisions of the FLSA,[20] injunctions, and consent judgements are being emphasized for cases in which child labor violations are found. Civil money penalties—"fines" computed in proportion to the severity of the violations—are assessed to affect the future compliance behavior of employers. The child-labor civil money penalty system now provides for a fine of $10,000 for each violation contributing to the death or serious injury of a minor.[21] The FLSA also contains criminal sanctions of up to 6 months imprisonment after a second conviction for violations of child labor regulations.

The second component of the compliance strategy is to educate all those who affect teen employment—employers, parents, teachers, other government agencies, and the working teens

themselves—about the child labor provisions and the importance of compliance. In June of 2000, the Wage and Hour Division of the U.S. Department of Labor will launch its fifth annual *Work Safe This Summer* education campaign, timed to reach both young workers and employers at the end of the school year when the number of teen workers swells. Concurrently, the Department's agricultural initiative, *Fair Harvest/Safe Harvest* will continue to provide hired farmworkers with important information about their rights in the workplace. This bilingual campaign also includes a colorful children's book designed to teach safety on the farm in an appealing and easily understood manner.

The Department continues to make available over the Internet important information about the child labor provisions. The Wage and Hour Division's *Youth Home Page* is designed to teach elementary school children about child labor and workplace safety. Extensive compliance information, including all the Federal child labor regulations, also is available on the Internet. In December 1998, the Department's *elaws* system—an interactive electronic information source—was expanded to include the child labor laws. Modules designed for employers, parents, teens, and other interested parties provide important information in a quick and user-friendly manner.

The Wage and Hour Division seeks to create partnerships with all parties that can contribute to increasing and maintaining compliance with the child labor provisions to help keep working children safe and in school. The Division's partners include employers, employer associations, child labor advocacy groups, community-based groups, and other government bodies. Some partnership agreements are the result of enforcement efforts or litigation, but most spring from the voluntary efforts of employers and other organizations coming together with the common goal of protecting young workers.

The National Institute for Occupational Safety and Health (NIOSH) and the National Consumers League have

been important partners in the *Work Safe This Summer* and *Fair Harvest/ Safe Harvest* campaigns since their inceptions. In addition, the Department of Labor is working closely with NIOSH to develop more effective interventions that better protect young workers and help prevent teen occupational injuries and deaths. The Department also is partnering with State Departments of Labor, including them in the strategic planning process, to promote coordinated enforcement and educational outreach activities. Enhanced coordination and cooperation between Federal and State agencies can only strengthen the effectiveness of efforts to increase compliance.

Further, the Wage and Hour Division also is seeking to create "corporate compliance partnerships" with those employers that agree to take extraordinary, proactive steps toward ensuring the safety and well-being of their young workers. Important national partnerships have already been forged with such enterprises as Kmart; H. J. Heinz; Toys "R" Us; Sears, Roebuck and Company; Newman's Own; and Smith Food and Drug Centers, Inc.

By heightening public awareness of youth employment issues and the Department's commitment to ensuring that safe and positive work experiences are available for teens, the Wage and Hour Division fosters an environment that encourages compliance with the child labor laws. Public awareness also can stimulate interest and, it is hoped, research in such areas as injury prevention, the effects of teen employment on academic performance, and identification of hazardous occupations.

Child labor enforcement trends

Recorded child labor violations were on a steep increase in the late 1980s. In response to this trend, the Department of Labor and several States took aggressive action, and there appears to have been an increase in child labor compliance over the last decade. The U.S. Department of Labor believes that its comprehensive compliance strategy is making a difference.

The Wage and Hour Division's enforcement experience suggests that fewer young people who work are working in violation of the child labor provisions. For example, despite the expenditure of a comparable proportion of enforcement resources on child labor compliance, the total number of investigations in which the Division found child labor violations decreased from a high of 5,889 in 1990 to 1,273 in 1998. The number of investigations in agriculture that found child labor violations likewise fell from 138 in 1990 to 33 in 1998. The number of young workers whose employment was in violation of the Federal child labor provisions, which reached nearly 40,000 in 1990, dropped to 5,500 in 1998. Even more indicative of increased compliance is the fact that the number of teens found illegally employed *per case* dropped from 6.8 in 1990 to 4.5 in 1998.

This trend in Federal enforcement data is supported by independent research. Douglas Kruse, in a study conducted for the *Associated Press*, derived estimates suggesting that, despite a significant increase in the *population* of working age youths—the "baby boom echo"—the proportion of youths who are illegally employed has dropped nearly 40 percent, from 1.3 percent in the 1970s to about 0.8 percent in the 1990s.[22]

It appears that the Nation's teens also are "working safer" than they did earlier in this decade. Data compiled by the National Institute for Occupational Safety and Health indicate that the risk of injury to working teens, as measured by cases treated in emergency rooms, decreased more than 10 percent between 1992 and 1996.[23] As noted in chapter 6 of this report, there was a 49-percent cumulative decrease in the number of injuries resulting in lost workdays to workers 17 years of age and younger from 1992 to 1997.

Such trends are encouraging, but we cannot become complacent. First and foremost, child labor remains a safety issue—and it is still the case that too many children are injured and killed on the job. NIOSH, using data from the National Electronic Injury Surveillance System, estimates that between 210,000 and 315,000 adolescents are injured on the job annually.[24]

As discussed in chapter 6, data from the BLS Survey of Occupational Injuries and Illnesses show an estimated 11,248 cases of injuries resulting in lost workdays to workers 17 and under in 1997. On average, according to the Census of Fatal Occupational Injuries, also discussed in chapter 6, 67 youths died on the job annually during the years 1992-97.[25]

Child labor is also an education issue. We must ensure that our youths, this country's most precious asset, find positive and safe work experiences that complement, rather than compete with, the educational process.

This chapter was contributed by Art Kerschner, Jr., leader, Child Labor and Special Employment Team, Employment Standards Administration.

[1] Wage and Hour and Public Contracts Division, *Child Labor Laws Historical Development* (Washington, U.S. Department of Labor, 1968), p. 2.

[2] Bureau of Labor Statistics, *Report on Conditions of Women and Child Wage-Earners in the United States* (61G, 2S, Senate Doc. 645, 1909).

[3] For a more detailed history of child labor in America, see Wage and Hour and Public Contracts Division, *Child Labor Laws.*

[4] *Protecting Youth at Work* (Washington, Institute of Medicine/National Research Council, 1998), p. 27.

[5] *Protecting Youth at Work*, p. 25.

[6] E. Greenberger and G. Steinberg, *When Teenagers Work: The Psychological and Social Costs of Adolescent Employment* (New York, Basic Books, 1986).

[7] Janice Windau, E. Sygnatur, and G. Toscano, "Profile of Work Injuries Incurred by Young Workers," *Monthly Labor Review*, June 1999, pp. 3-10.

[8] *New ILO Child Labour Convention Receives First Ratification,* ILO/99/30 (Geneva, International Labor Organization, September 1999).

[9] A covered enterprise consists of the related activities performed through unified operation or common control by any person or persons for a common business purpose and 1) whose annual gross volume of sales made or business done is not less than $500,000 (exclusive of excise taxes at the retail level that are separately stated); or 2) that is engaged in the operation of a hospital, an institution primarily engaged in the care of the sick, the aged, or the mentally ill who reside on the premises; a school for mentally or physically disabled or gifted children; a preschool, an elementary or secondary school, or an institution of higher education (whether operated for profit or not for profit); or 3) that is an activity of a public agency.

[10] The following types of youth employment are exempt from the child labor provisions of the FLSA: 1) children under 16 who are employed by their parents in occupations other than mining, manufacturing, or those declared hazardous by the Secretary of Labor; 2) children employed as actors or performers in motion pictures or theatrical, radio, or television productions; 3) children engaged in the delivery of newspapers to the consumer; 4) home-workers engaged in the making of wreaths composed of natural holly, pine, cedar, or other evergreens.

[11] Farmworkers who are employed by agricultural employers who did not, during any calendar quarter during the preceding calendar year, use more than 500 man-days of agricultural labor are exempt from the FLSA minimum wage requirements. This roughly equates to about seven employees in any quarter.

[12] A court injunction currently blocks the Department from issuing these waivers because employers are unable to provide absolute proof that the health or well-being of young workers would be at zero risk from exposure to pesticides or other chemicals.

[13] Agricultural employment is exempted from or is not listed among the covered sectors in the child labor laws of Alabama, Delaware (nonhazardous employment), Georgia, Kansas, Kentucky, Louisiana, Maryland, Mississippi, Montana, Nebraska (covers only work in beet fields), North Carolina, Oklahoma, Rhode Is-

land, Tennessee, Texas, West Virginia, and Wyoming.

[14] New Jersey, New York, Ohio, South Carolina, Vermont, Virginia, Washington, and Wisconsin.

[15] Arkansas, California, Colorado, Florida, Michigan, New Hampshire, Pennsylvania, and Washington.

[16] Alaska, Colorado, Connecticut, Florida, Iowa, Michigan, Minnesota, New Jersey, Oregon, Utah, Virginia, and Washington.

[17] D. Castillo, D. Landen, and L. Layne, "Occupational Injury Deaths of 16- and 17-Year-Olds in the United States," *American Journal of Public Health*, April 1994.

[18] In a press release dated January 20, 1999, the Insurance Institute for Highway Safety reported that 24 States have enacted some form of graduated licensing since 1994.

[19] Only one standard—that dealing with exposure to ionizing radiation—establishes a lower permissible exposure level for workers under 18 years of age than for adults.

[20] The FLSA bars the shipment or delivery for shipment in commerce of "hot goods" produced in an establishment in or about which oppressive child labor is being employed or was employed in the past 30 days.

[21] The Department of Labor has proposed, in a Notice of Proposed Rulemaking published in the *Federal Register* on December 12, 1998, to increase the maximum child labor civil money penalty to $11,000 (63 FR71405). This proposal was made to meet the requirements of the Federal Civil Penalties Inflation Adjustment Act of 1990. A final rule has yet to be promulgated.

[22] D. Kruse, *Illegal Child Labor in the United States* (New Brunswick, NJ, School of Management and Labor Relations, Rutgers University and National Bureau of Economic Research, November 1997). However, it should also be noted that, over the period from the late 1970s to the late 1990s, the percentage of 15- to 17-years-olds who worked declined from 30 to 25 in school months and from 43 to 34 in summer months.

See chapter 4, table 4.1 in this report.

[23] NIOSH reported rates for work-related injuries treated in emergency departments for 16- to 17-year-old males and females in 1996 to be 6.0 and 3.9 injuries per 100 full-time equivalent workers, respectively. See D. Castillo, L. Davis, and D. Wegman, "Young Workers," *Occupational Medicine: State of the Art Reviews*, July-September 1999. NIOSH reported work-related injuries treated in emergency departments for 16- to 17-year-old males and females in 1992 to be 7.0 and 4.4 injuries per 100 full-time equivalent workers, respectively. See L. Layne, D. Castillo, N. Stout, and P. Cutlip, "Adolescent Occupational Injuries Requiring Hospital Emergency Department Treatment: A Nationally Representative Sample," *American Journal of Public Health*, vol. 84, 1994, pp. 657–60.

[24] Castillo and others, "Young Workers."

[25] Michael H. Cimini, "Fatal Injuries and Young Workers," *Compensation and Working Conditions*, Summer 1999, pp. 27-29.

Chapter 3.
A Detailed Look at Employment of Youths Aged 12 to 15

Introduction

This chapter examines employment patterns of youths using data from the first interview of the National Longitudinal Survey of Youth 1997 (NLSY97). The NLSY97 was designed specifically to collect a wide range of information on youths in the United States. It provides insight into their labor market experiences, demographic and family characteristics, and participation in school-to-work programs, as well as many other aspects of their lives. The NLSY97 provides an in-depth focus on a cohort of youths who were between the ages of 12 and 16 on December 31, 1996. The first interview will be followed by annual interviews to develop longitudinal data. NLSY97 data complement data from the Current Population Survey (CPS), a monthly survey of households that provides data on trends over time but does not track specific age cohorts. CPS information on employment trends of youths aged 15 to 17 is described in chapter 4.

In 1997, a nationally representative sample of 9,022 young men and women who were born between January 1, 1980, and December 31, 1984, were interviewed in the NLSY97. Thus, respondents were between the ages of 12 and 17 at the time of this first interview. In this chapter, the employment patterns of the young persons while they were aged 14 and 15 are described in detail, followed by a less-detailed look at work among youths while they were aged 12. Finally, participation in school-to-work programs by youths in the ninth grade or higher is discussed.

The NLSY97 survey instrument

The NLSY97 survey instrument uses several tools to identify and classify youth employment. It is widely understood that many youths first enter the labor market through casual employment arrangements. These "freelance" arrangements are characterized by doing one or more tasks, often on an as-needed basis or for multiple employers. For example, babysitting and lawn-mowing services often are provided in this way. By contrast, "employee" jobs, as defined in the NLSY97, are characterized by an ongoing relationship between the young person and his or her particular employer. The NLSY97 was specifically designed to pick up both types of employment. The survey asked detailed questions about all of the "employee" and "freelance" jobs held since one's 14th birthday. Questions about "any jobs" held since the age of 12 were asked of those aged 12 and 13.

What percentage of youths work at ages 14 and 15?

This analysis focuses on employment during the years that youths were 14 and 15. Because very few youths in the NLSY97 sample had turned 17 by the time of their interview, the employment history for the entire year they were aged 16 was collected for only a small sample. In order to determine whether the youths did any paid work since turning 14, they were first introduced to the concepts of employee jobs and freelance jobs. The interviewer then asked them about these jobs, filling in a calendar of weeks since their 14th birthday.[1]

Well over half (57 percent) of interviewed youths reported having held some type of job while they were aged 14. (See chart 3.1.) Freelance jobs

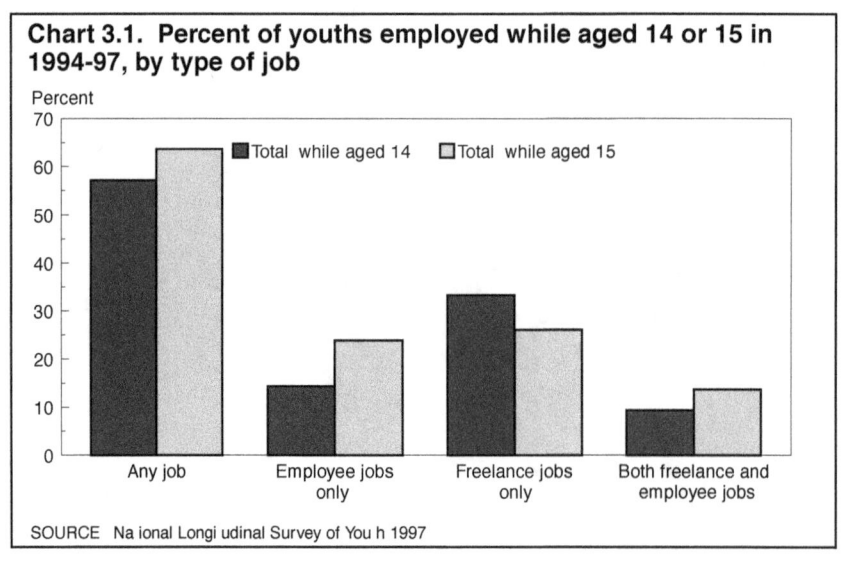

Chart 3.1. Percent of youths employed while aged 14 or 15 in 1994-97, by type of job

SOURCE National Longitudinal Survey of Youth 1997

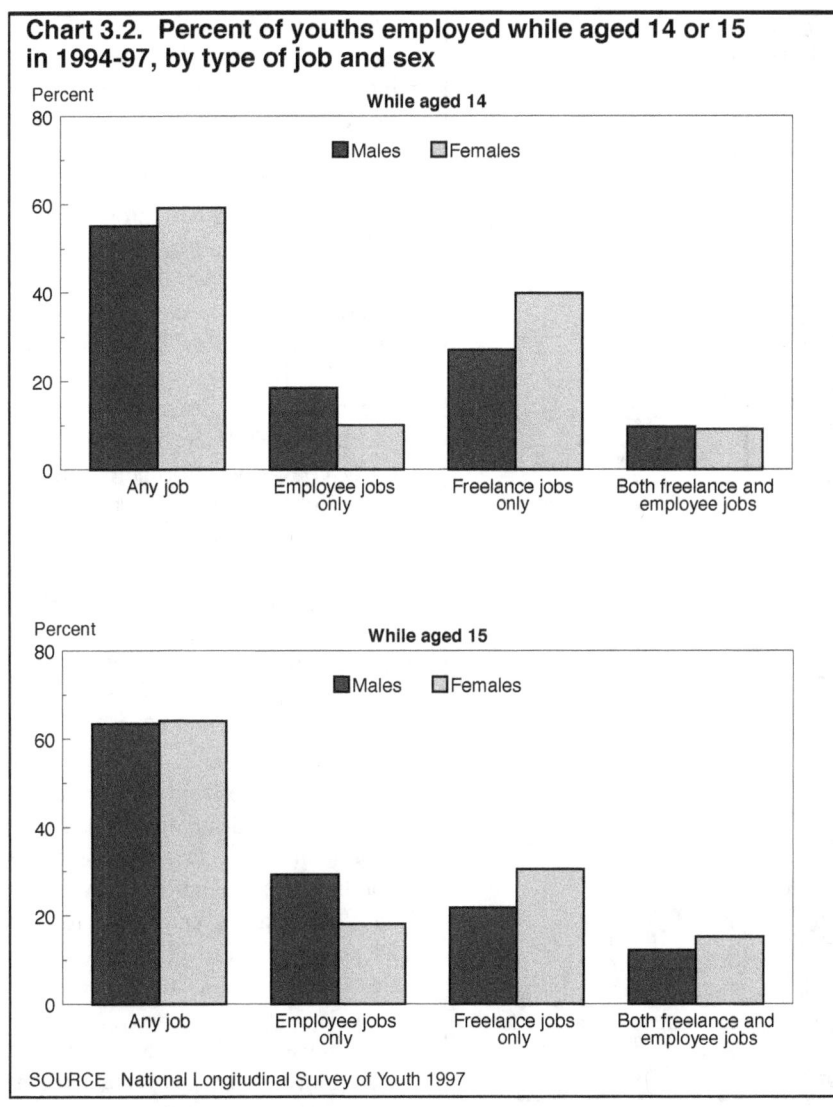

Chart 3.2. Percent of youths employed while aged 14 or 15 in 1994-97, by type of job and sex

Percent

While aged 14

■Males □Females

| Any job | Employee jobs only | Freelance jobs only | Both freelance and employee jobs |

Percent

While aged 15

■Males □Females

| Any job | Employee jobs only | Freelance jobs only | Both freelance and employee jobs |

SOURCE National Longitudinal Survey of Youth 1997

were held more often by 14-year-olds than were employee jobs. A total of 43 percent held a freelance job at age 14, while 24 percent held an employee job. There was some overlap among the groups. About 9 percent of all youths held at least one of each type of job during the year they were 14.

Employment was more common at age 15 than at age 14, as young people increasingly took on employee jobs and continued to do freelance work. Overall, 64 percent of youths worked in some type of job while they were aged 15. Forty percent of the young people interviewed had done freelance work—about the same proportion as among 14-year-olds. Nearly as many—38 percent—had an ongoing employment relationship (employee job) while they were aged 15, up from

24 percent while aged 14. Among 15-year-olds, 14 percent held at least one of each type of job during the year.

At age 14, female youths were slightly more likely than male youths to work—59 percent versus 55 percent, respectively. At age 15, the rates were essentially the same (63 percent versus 64 percent). There were differences in the types of jobs held, however. At both ages, males were more likely than females to hold employee jobs, while females were more likely to do freelance work. (See chart 3.2.)

White youths were more likely than either black or Hispanic youths to have held employee or freelance jobs when they were 14 or 15.[2] (See chart 3.3.) Nearly two-thirds (64 percent) of white youths held one or the other type of job at age 14, compared with 43 and

41 percent of black and Hispanic youths, respectively. Both whites and Hispanics were more likely to work at age 15 than at age 14, but race/ethnicity differences in the percentages of youths employed persisted. Differences may have stemmed from labor market difficulties for black and Hispanic youths. Data from the CPS discussed in chapter 4 show that black and Hispanic youths are much more likely to be unemployed (actively seeking work) than are white youths.

NLSY97 data also show that youths in lower income households tend to work less than do those in households with higher incomes. Table 3.1 shows the percentage of youths with employee jobs crossed by the incomes of their households. As shown, youths in households with incomes below $25,000 annually were less likely to work than were those in households with higher incomes. Twenty-one percent of the young people in the lowest-income group held employee jobs when they were 14, compared with between 25 and 27 percent of those whose households had incomes in the three higher groups. The same pattern occurred for youths aged 15: 32 percent in the lowest household income group held employee jobs, compared with between 40 and 42 percent in the higher income groups. As we will see in chapter 4, CPS data also show lower employment-to-population ratios for youths in families with relatively low income. The NLSY97 data also show that, at age 14 (but not at age 15), youths in two-parent families were more likely to work than were those in families headed by a female parent. Among 14-year-olds, 61 percent of those in two-parent families held a job, compared with 54 percent in families headed by women.[3]

It is not clear why young people in households with lower incomes are less likely to be employed than are those in households with higher incomes, but the intersection between family income and family structure may affect youth employment rates. Households with lower incomes may have fewer adults than do households

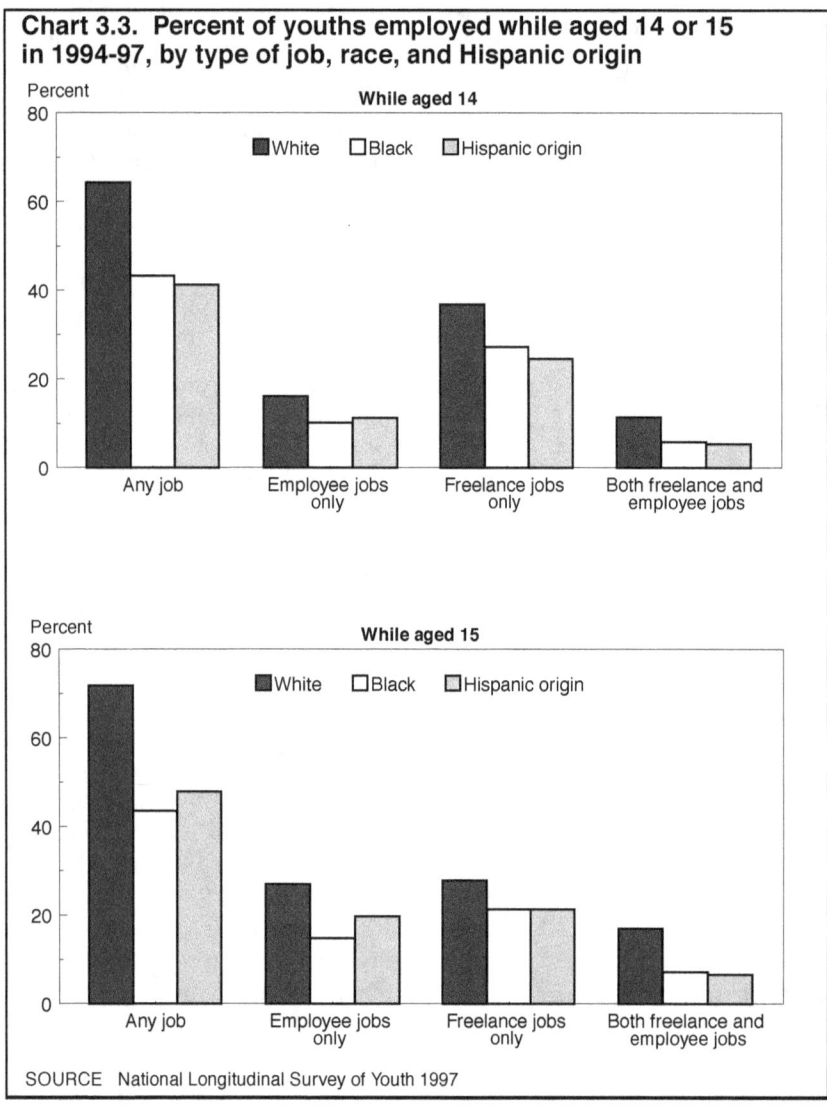

Chart 3.3. Percent of youths employed while aged 14 or 15 in 1994-97, by type of job, race, and Hispanic origin

Percent

While aged 14

80

■White □Black ▨Hispanic origin

60

40

20

0

Any job | Employee jobs only | Freelance jobs only | Both freelance and employee jobs

Percent

While aged 15

80

■White □Black ▨Hispanic origin

60

40

20

0

Any job | Employee jobs only | Freelance jobs only | Both freelance and employee jobs

SOURCE National Longitudinal Survey of Youth 1997

with higher incomes. Youths in households with fewer adults may have more responsibilities in the home and be less available to work outside the home for pay. Those from families with lower incomes may have less access to a car or to adults available to drive them to a job. Poorer communities also tend to have higher unemployment rates; thus, the youths may have a harder time finding or keeping jobs locally.

At ages 14 and 15, foreign-born youths were less likely to hold a job than were the native born. Among foreign-born youths, 43 percent held a job at some point while they were aged 14, compared with 60 percent of their native-born counterparts. At age 15, 51 percent of foreign-born youths held a job, compared with 67 percent of the native born (numbers not shown in table).[4] The lower employment rates for foreign-born youths may reflect factors that could reduce their relative success at finding jobs. These might include problems speaking English, possession of relatively fewer job search skills in the U.S. labor market, fewer employment contacts, or employment discrimination. Data from the Current Population Survey for 15- to 17-year-olds show the same employment pattern between foreign- and native-born youths, as discussed in chapter 4.

How much do youths work at ages 14 and 15?

How much youths *should* work has received considerable policy attention in recent years. Gaining some work ex-

perience during the high school years is viewed by some as valuable in easing the transition from school to work. Working too many hours, however, also is viewed as potentially harmful to academic studies. Data from the NLSY97 can be used to provide recent information on weeks and hours that youths work while in school. Chapter 7 further explores outcomes of youth employment using data from the NLSY79 interviews conducted between 1979 and 1996.

The NLSY97 calendar-based method of collecting information on employee jobs enables researchers to identify the specific weeks during which youths worked in employee jobs. Chart 3.4 shows the proportion of youths who worked during different times of the year—school-year weeks, summer weeks, or both—at ages 14 and 15.[5] A total of 18 percent of 14-year-olds worked either during the school-year weeks only or during both school-year and summer weeks. This represented the large majority of youths who had employee jobs at that age. Among 15-year-olds, a total of 31 percent worked in employee jobs that included work during the school year.

While aged 14 and 15, male youths were more likely than female youths to work during the school term. Among 14-year-olds, 22 percent of males and 14 percent of females worked during the school year; among 15-year-olds, 35 percent of males and 28 percent of females held school-term jobs. At both 14 and 15, whites were more likely to work during the school year than were blacks or Hispanics. (See table 3.2.) At age 14 only, youths in two-parent families were more likely to work during the school year than were those in families headed by women.

Particular concern centers on the intensity of work by youths during the school year. Intensity can be measured in terms of both weeks and hours of work. Looking at the overall population of 14-year-olds, we find that 8 percent worked during the school year and averaged 15 or more hours per

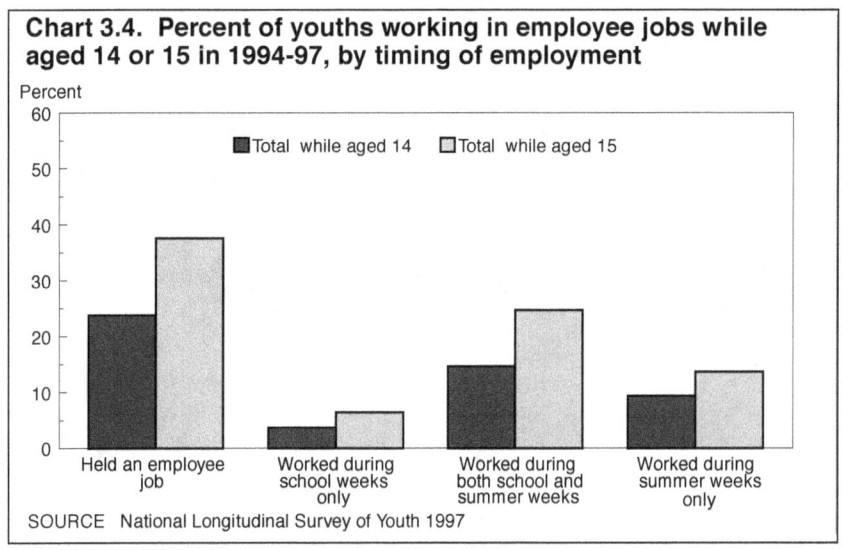

Chart 3.4. Percent of youths working in employee jobs while aged 14 or 15 in 1994-97, by timing of employment

Percent

■ Total while aged 14   □ Total while aged 15

SOURCE National Longitudinal Survey of Youth 1997

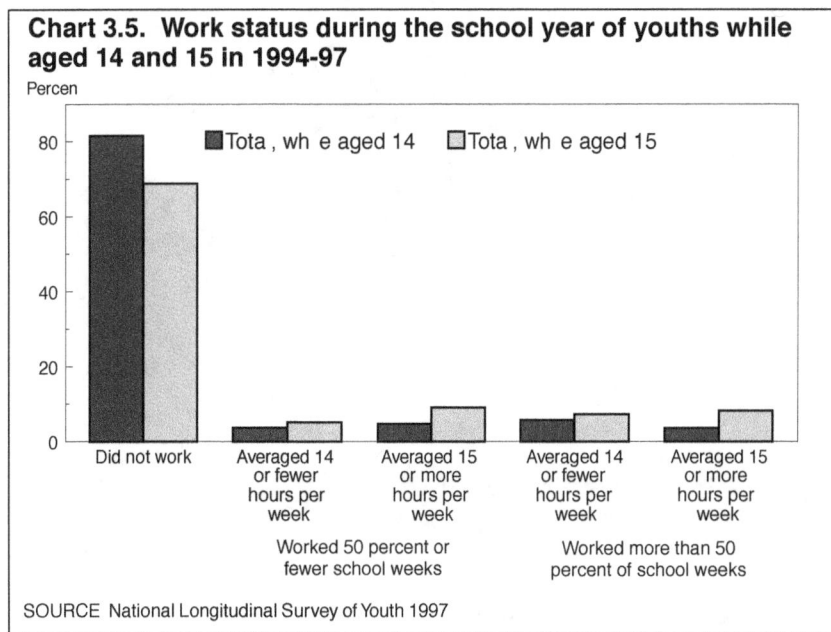

Chart 3.5. Work status during the school year of youths while aged 14 and 15 in 1994-97

Percen

■ Tota , wh e aged 14   □ Tota , wh e aged 15

Worked 50 percent or fewer school weeks

Worked more than 50 percent of school weeks

SOURCE National Longitudinal Survey of Youth 1997

week during academic weeks in which they worked.[6] Nine percent of all 14-year-olds worked more than half of the weeks during the school year. Note that the above two groups are not mutually exclusive. Among 15-year-olds, 17 percent worked during the school year and averaged 15 or more hours per week. Sixteen percent worked more than half of the school-year weeks. (See chart 3.5.)

Male youths were more likely than female youths to work 15 or more hours per week at employee jobs during the school year at these ages. Among 15-year-olds, 20 percent of males reported such work, compared with 15 percent of their female counterparts. Male youths also worked more weeks during the school year than did their female peers. Among 15-year-olds, 18 percent of males worked at employee jobs for more than half of the weeks in the school year, compared with 13 percent of females. (See table 3.3.)

These measures of intensity—hours per week and the percent of school weeks worked—also were greater for white youths than for black or Hispanic youths at these ages. Among white 15-year-olds, 21 percent worked at employee jobs for 15 or more hours per week, compared with 9 percent of blacks and 12 percent of Hispanics.

Similarly, 19 percent of whites aged 15 worked at employee jobs for more than half of school-year weeks, compared with only 6 to 7 percent of blacks and Hispanics.

Only 4 percent of 14-year-olds can be classified as working at high intensity relative to their peers—15 or more hours per week *and* more than half of school-year weeks. Eight percent of 15-year-olds were in this category. Male youths were more likely than female youths to work such a schedule at these ages: 5 percent of males aged 14 and 10 percent of those aged 15 had such a schedule, compared with 2 percent and 6 percent of females at these ages. Ten percent of white youths worked 15 or more hours per week over a majority of school-year weeks while aged 15, compared with only 3 percent of black and 4 percent of Hispanic youths.

An alternative view of the same data on intensity is provided by looking at the schedules of those who actually *held jobs* during the school year at age 14 or 15. This view eliminates the effect of lower overall participation rates on the examination of work schedules. Some noteworthy effects are found with respect to race and ethnicity. While whites are more likely to work overall while aged 14, employed black youths worked longer hours at this age than did whites or Hispanics. Sixty percent of working black youths worked 15 or more hours per week during the school year, compared with 44 percent of working whites and 46 percent of working Hispanics. However, among 15-year-olds, employed white, black, and Hispanic youths were about equally likely to average 15 or more hours of work per week. As was the case for the overall groups of 14- and 15-year-olds, whites who are employed at these ages are generally more likely to work during a majority of school weeks than are their black or Hispanic counterparts.[7]

Where young people work
The NLSY97 obtained data on the industries of employee jobs in which

youths worked and on the occupations that they held while they were aged 14 and 15. The job in which they worked the most weeks at each age is discussed here. Employee jobs and freelance jobs are described separately.

Employee jobs. As shown in chart 3.6, among youths with employee jobs, the large majority—two-thirds at age 14 and three-quarters at age 15—held jobs in either the retail or services industries. Between ages 14 and 15, the proportion working in retail trade increased from 29 to 45 percent. Many of those employed in this industry worked in eating and drinking establishments. The top 10 industries that employed 14- and 15-year-olds are shown in descending order in table 3.4. After eating and drinking places, entertainment and recreation services industries and construction were most likely to employ these young workers.

Tables 3.5 and 3.6 highlight industry employment patterns by gender. Among 14-year-olds, 5 of the top 10 industries were the same for males and females. These included eating and drinking establishments, entertainment and recreation services, and the construction industry. Landscape and horticultural services, livestock production, and automotive repair were some of the industries on the top 10 list for male youths that were not on the list for their female peers. (Employment in agriculture is examined in detail in chapter 5.) The list for female youths included work for child daycare services, religious organizations, and building services. Between ages 14 and 15, employment in eating and drinking places became increasingly common for both males and females, while working in agricultural and landscaping services declined for males and working in private households declined for females.

Occupational patterns provide a clearer picture of the tasks that young people perform. Chart 3.7 shows that youths are spread among quite a few occupational categories. The largest overall occupational group for workers at ages 14 and 15 was service oc-

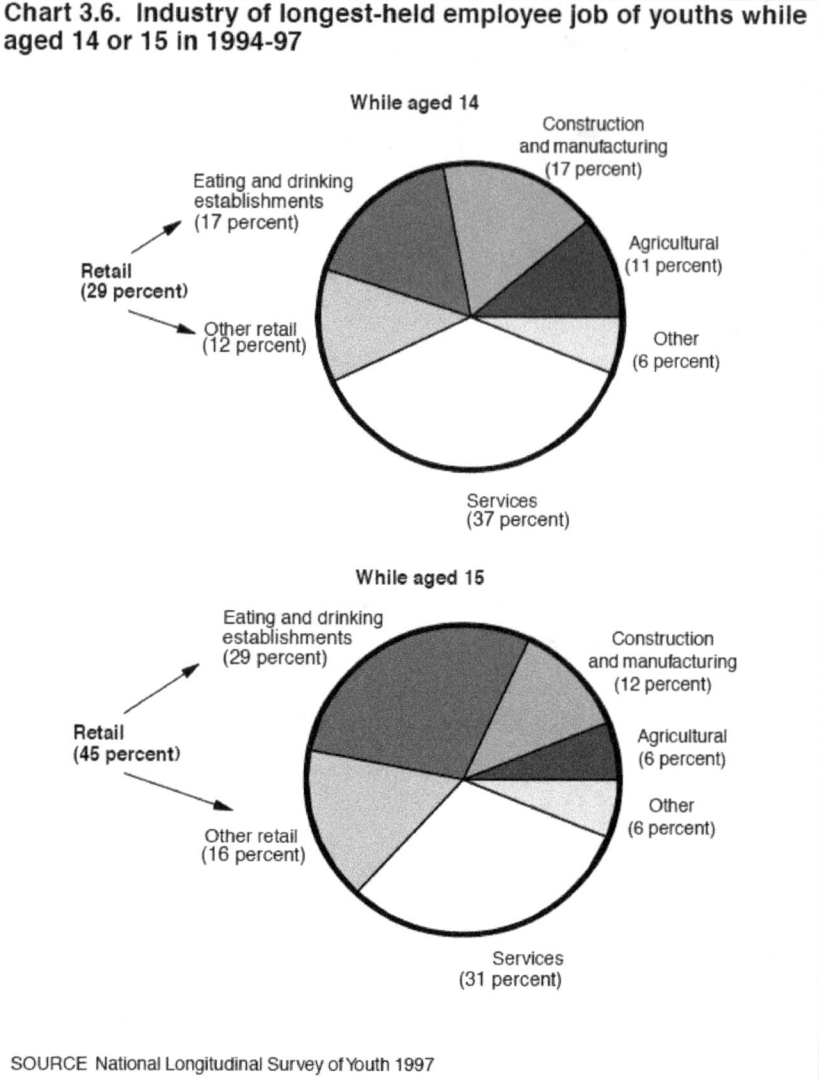

Chart 3.6. Industry of longest-held employee job of youths while aged 14 or 15 in 1994-97

While aged 14

Eating and drinking establishments (17 percent)

Construction and manufacturing (17 percent)

Agricultural (11 percent)

Retail (29 percent)

Other retail (12 percent)

Other (6 percent)

Services (37 percent)

While aged 15

Eating and drinking establishments (29 percent)

Construction and manufacturing (12 percent)

Agricultural (6 percent)

Retail (45 percent)

Other (6 percent)

Other retail (16 percent)

Services (31 percent)

SOURCE National Longitudinal Survey of Youth 1997

cupations, employing 33 percent of youths aged 14 (with employee jobs) and 37 percent of those aged 15. Food preparation and service jobs—such as cooks, waiters, and waitresses—are among the service occupations frequently held by young workers. Among both 14- and 15-year-olds, sales jobs (including cashiers) were also frequently held by youths. Fifteen percent of those with employee jobs at age 14, and 19 percent of those with such jobs at age 15, held sales positions. Table 3.7 shows the top 10 occupations held by youths at each age.

There are noteworthy differences in occupations of male and female youths. Tables 3.8 and 3.9 show that both males and females often work as

janitors or cleaners, cooks, and cashiers. The top occupation for females was cashiers, employing almost 11 percent of 14-year-olds and 16 percent of 15-year-olds. Employed male 14-year-olds are most likely to work as janitors or cleaners; at age 15, they are most often employed as cooks. Male youths are more likely than are their female peers to work as stock handlers or laborers or to do lawn work ("grounds-keepers"), while female youths are more likely to perform childcare or to work as cashiers, receptionists, or office clerks.

Freelance jobs. Among youths who held freelance jobs, babysitting and yard work were by far the most popu-

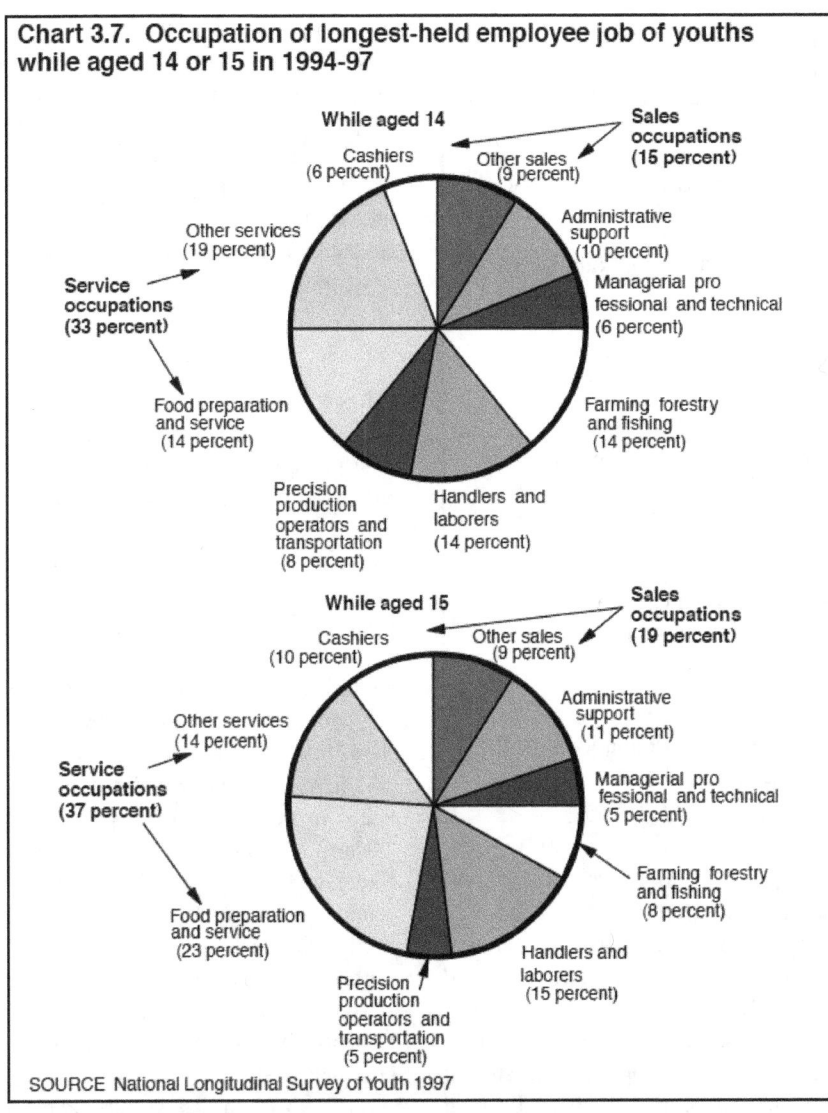

Chart 3.7. Occupation of longest-held employee job of youths while aged 14 or 15 in 1994-97

While aged 14

Sales occupations (15 percent)
- Cashiers (6 percent)
- Other sales (9 percent)
- Administrative support (10 percent)
- Managerial pro fessional and technical (6 percent)
- Farming forestry and fishing (14 percent)
- Handlers and laborers (14 percent)
- Precision production operators and transportation (8 percent)

Service occupations (33 percent)
- Other services (19 percent)
- Food preparation and service (14 percent)

While aged 15

Sales occupations (19 percent)
- Cashiers (10 percent)
- Other sales (9 percent)
- Administrative support (11 percent)
- Managerial pro fessional and technical (5 percent)
- Farming forestry and fishing (8 percent)
- Handlers and laborers (15 percent)
- Precision production operators and transportation (5 percent)

Service occupations (37 percent)
- Other services (14 percent)
- Food preparation and service (23 percent)

SOURCE National Longitudinal Survey of Youth 1997

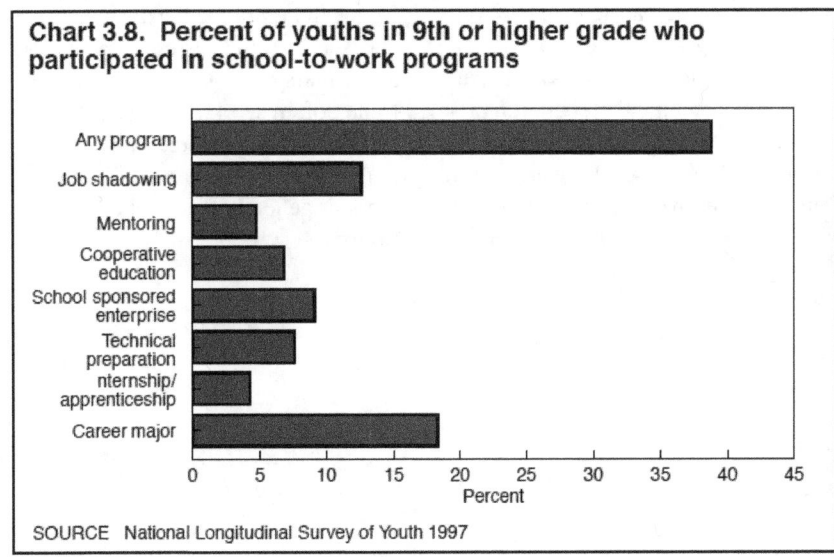

Chart 3.8. Percent of youths in 9th or higher grade who participated in school-to-work programs

- Any program
- Job shadowing
- Mentoring
- Cooperative education
- School sponsored enterprise
- Technical preparation
- Internship/ apprenticeship
- Career major

Percent

SOURCE National Longitudinal Survey of Youth 1997

lar types.[8] As reported in table 3.10, of the more than 4 in 10 young people who did some freelance work at age 14, 62 percent reported babysitting and 38 percent reported doing lawn work. Patterns were similar among 15-year-olds who held freelance jobs. Gender differences in freelance employment were dramatic. More than 90 percent of working female youths at both ages 14 and 15 reported having done some babysitting. Among male youths with freelance jobs, only 25 percent of 14-year-olds and 20 percent of 15-year-olds reported doing such work. By contrast, nearly three-quarters of working male youths reported doing yard work at each age, compared with only 1 in 10 female youths. White youths are more likely than black or Hispanic youths to hold freelance jobs. Among those who did freelance work at age 14 or 15, race differences in the types of freelance jobs held were not dramatic; at both ages, whites were somewhat more likely to babysit than were blacks.

Employment while aged 12

The NLSY97 asked a different set of questions of youths aged 13 and under as of the date of the interview. These questions determined whether the respondents had held "any jobs" since their 12th birthday. They did not distinguish between freelance and employee work arrangements. For youths who were aged 13 at the time of the interview, a look at the entire 12 months during which they were aged 12 was possible.[9]

Table 3.11 indicates that work starts at young ages. Half of the 13-year-olds interviewed reported having some work experience while they were aged 12, compared with 57 percent of youths who reported having any type of job at age 14. Many of these very young workers did either babysitting or yard work.[10] Among males aged 12, a quarter reported doing some babysitting during the year, and two-thirds reported doing yard work. Among females, 85 percent did some babysitting and 14 percent did yard work.

Participation in school-to-work programs

School-to-work programs are designed to help youths prepare for and make the transition to the world of work.

School-to-Work Programs	
Job shadowing	Spending time following workers at a worksite
Mentoring	Being matched with an individual in an occupation
Cooperative education	Combining academic and vocational studies with a job in a related field
School-sponsored enterprise	Producing goods or services for sale to or use by others
Technical preparation	Participating in a planned program of study with a defined career focus that links secondary and postsecondary education
Internship or apprenticeship	Working for an employer to learn about a particular occupation or industry
Career major	Taking a defined sequence of courses based upon an occupational goal

The NLSY97 included specific questions about participation in such programs by youths in the 9th or higher grades.[11] These programs include job shadowing, mentoring, and cooperative education, among others. (See box for program descriptions.)

As shown in chart 3.8, nearly 4 in 10 young people participated in some type of school-to-work program. Taking a defined set of courses based on an occupational goal—having a "career major"—was the most frequent program, with 18 percent of youths participating. Thirteen percent of youths did some job shadowing and

nine percent participated in a school-sponsored enterprise. The least-used programs were mentoring (5 percent) and internships or apprenticeships (4 percent).

The incidence of participation in school-to-work programs was similar for male and female youths, with about 39 percent participating in at least one type of program. (See table 3.12.) Males were slightly more likely to participate in a technical preparation program, and females were more likely to be in a job shadowing program. Black youths were more likely than white or Hispanic youths to participate

in a program—46 percent versus 39 and 32 percent, respectively. Specifically, blacks were more likely to participate in cooperative education, technical preparation, internships or apprenticeships, and career major programs. The incidence of program participation did not vary much by household income.

Summary

At age 12, half of American youths engage in some type of work activity. The percentage of youths who work increases from age 14 to age 15, and young people tend to move from freelance work—such as babysitting and lawn mowing—into more formal, ongoing employment relationships. Work is very common during the school year and the majority of youths with employee jobs work during both the school year and the summer.

There are gender and race differences in the employment patterns of 14- and 15-year-olds. Males are more likely to have employee jobs, while females are more likely to do freelance work. Whites are more likely to be employed than are either blacks or Hispanics; they also are more likely to work during both the school and summer months.

At both 14 and 15, youths are most frequently employed in the retail trade and services industries. Many work as cashiers or as janitors or cleaners. Males often work as construction laborers or in lawn care, while their female peers often perform child care or work as general office clerks or receptionists.

This chapter was contributed by Donna Rothstein, a research economist, and Diane Herz, an economist, both with the Bureau of Labor Statistics. The authors would like to thank Michael Horrigan for helpful comments and Alexander Eidelman and Julie Yates for excellent research assistance.

[1] Start and stop dates, as well as information on within-job gaps, are gathered for all employee jobs that respondents held since age 14. Start and stop dates also are gathered for all freelance jobs. However, gaps within freelance jobs are not collected due to the sporadic nature of these jobs. Thus, the definition of freelance jobs while aged 14 (while aged 15) used in the tables and charts that follow depends on whether the period between the start and stop dates of any freelance job spans any of the weeks during which the respondent was 14 (15). If, for example, the freelance job began before the respondent turned 15 and ended after the respondent turned 16, then the respondent would be counted as working in a freelance job at age 15. This may overstate the incidence of working at freelance jobs among youths.

[2] The race and ethnic categories used in this chapter, based on NLSY97 data, are different from those used in other BLS surveys. In other surveys, estimates usually are published for whites, blacks, and persons of Hispanic origin. These groups are not mutually exclusive because Hispanics are considered to be an ethnic group rather than a racial group and can be included in any racial category. In this chapter, estimates are reported for three mutually exclusive groups: non-Hispanic whites, non-Hispanic blacks, and Hispanics. Although these groups are mutually exclusive, they are not exhaustive. American Indians, Alaskan natives, and Asians and Pacific Islanders are included in the totals but are not shown separately because of the small number of sample members in these racial categories.

[3] There were not enough male-headed, one-parent families to examine youths from those families separately. Youths who were not living with a parent were the least likely to work while aged 14 and 15. Youths in this group lived with grandparents, foster parents, or in group quarters, or had other arrangements.

[4] The NLSY97 does not specifically ask whether the youth was foreign born. Our definition of foreign born is as follows: If the interviewed youth's biological mother first came to the United States in a year subsequent to the youth's year of birth, the youth is defined as "foreign born." If the youth's biological mother was born in the United States or first came to the United States in a year prior to the youth's birth, the youth is defined as "native born."

[5] Summer weeks are defined as those in June, July, and August. School weeks exclude those in June, July, and August, as well as the last week in December and the first week in January.

[6] Hours are defined according to the following methodology. Survey respondents report usual hours per week as of each employee job's stop date (or the interview date for ongoing jobs). Hours reported for each job are then back-filled to the job's start date. Each week during which the youth worked, then, has an hours total. Then, hours per week are averaged over all the academic weeks worked while the respondent was aged 14 or 15. Given this methodology, summer work hours are sometimes back-filled into school-year weeks, leading to a potential overstatement of average hours. For both 14- and 15-year-olds, about one-third (33 and 34 percent, respectively) of school-year weeks worked were back-filled with summer hours. Mean hours of work per week during school-year weeks that were back-filled with summer hours were 19 for 14-year-olds and 22 for 15-year-olds. Mean hours of work per week during school-year weeks that were back-filled with school-year hours were lower at 15 and 16 (14- and 15-year-olds, respectively).

[7] The sample size of foreign-born youths is not large enough to permit examination of work schedules by native- versus foreign-born status.

[8] It should be noted that the interviewer, when describing freelance jobs to youths, uses both babysitting and yard work as examples. Yard work includes mowing lawns, shoveling snow, landscaping, and gardening. If youths have more than one freelance job while these ages, they may be counted in both the babysitting and yard work columns of table 3.10.

[9] Examining employment for the full year during which the respondent was aged 13 was not possible, however, because youths who had turned 14 at the time of the survey were asked the more detailed questions about employment since the age of 14 that were discussed earlier.

[10] If youths have more than one work activity while aged 12, they may be counted in both the babysitting and yard work columns of table 3.11.

[11] The NLSY97 asks youths whether they have "ever" participated in each of the programs listed. Responses reflect the young respondents' perceptions of whether they have participated in such programs. No determination is made as to whether the particular school-to-work programs are actually offered at the respondent's (current or past) school.

Tab e 3.1. **Percent of youths employed while aged 14 or 15 in 1994-97, by type of job, sex, race, Hispanic origin, household income, and family structure**

Age in 1994 97 and characteristic	Percent employed					
	Any job	Any employee job	Any freelance job	Employee jobs only	Freelance jobs only	Both employee and freelance jobs
While aged 14						
Total	57 2	23 8	42 8	14 4	33 3	9 4
Sex						
Male	55 2	28 1	36 8	18 5	27 1	9 7
Female	59 2	19 3	49 1	10 1	39 9	9 2
Race and Hispanic origin						
White	64 3	27 5	48 3	16 1	36 8	11 4
Black	43 3	16 0	33 1	10 2	27 3	5 8
Hispanic origin	41 3	16 7	30 1	11 3	24 6	5 4
Household income						
Less than $25 000	48 6	20 5	34 7	13 9	28 1	6 6
$25 000 to 44 999	62 7	25 5	46 4	16 3	37 3	9 1
$45 000 to 69 999	63 0	26 5	49 3	13 6	36 5	12 9
$70 000 and over	63 5	25 0	49 5	13 9	38 5	11 0
Family structure						
Two parent family	61 0	25 6	46 0	15 0	35 4	10 6
Female parent family	53 9	21 4	40 3	13 6	32 6	7 8
Not living with parent	39 4	10 9	31 4	8 0	28 5	2 9
While aged 15						
Total	63 7	37 6	39 8	23 9	26 1	13 7
Sex						
Male	63 4	41 5	34 1	29 3	21 9	12 2
Female	64 1	33 5	45 8	18 2	30 6	15 3
Race and Hispanic origin						
White	71 8	44 0	44 8	27 0	27 9	17 0
Black	43 6	22 2	28 7	14 9	21 4	7 3
Hispanic origin	47 9	26 5	28 1	19 8	21 4	6 7
Household income						
Less than $25 000	52 3	32 3	30 9	21 4	20 0	10 9
$25 000 to 44 999	70 9	40 8	44 7	26 1	30 1	14 7
$45 000 to 69 999	69 4	39 8	46 9	22 5	29 6	17 3
$70 000 and over	75 6	42 2	49 4	26 2	33 4	16 0
Family structure						
Two parent family	67 3	38 6	43 0	24 2	28 7	14 3
Female parent family	63 6	38 2	40 2	23 4	25 4	14 8
Not living with parent	43 3	25 9	22 5	20 8	17 3	5 1

NOTE The National Longitudinal Survey of Youth 1997 con sists of young men and women who were aged 12 to 16 on De cember 31 1996 Race and Hispanic origin groups are mutually exclusive Totals include American ndians Alaskan Natives and Asians and Pacific slanders not shown separately "While aged 14" refers to the entire year between the individuals 14th and 15th birthdays The first 13 rows exclude individuals who were not yet 15 years of age when interviewed "While aged 15" refers to the entire year between the individuals 15th and 16th birthdays The last 13 rows exclude individuals who were not yet 16 years of age when interviewed

Tab e 3.2. **Percent of youths with an employee job while aged 14 and 15 in 1994-97, by timing of employment, sex, race, Hispanic origin, household income, and family structure**

Age in 1994-97 and characteristic	Percent with an employee job	Worked during school year weeks			Worked during summer weeks only
		Total	Worked during school year weeks only	Worked during both school year and summer weeks	
While aged 14					
Total	23 8	18 4	3 7	14 7	5 3
Sex					
Male	28 1	22 4	4 5	17 9	5 6
Female	19 3	14 2	2 8	11 4	5 0
Race and Hispanic origin					
White	27 5	22 1	3 9	18 2	5 3
Black	16 0	9 9	2 7	7 1	6 1
Hispanic origin	16 7	11 9	4 0	8 0	4 6
Household income					
Less than $25 000	20 5	15 2	3 3	11 9	5 3
$25 000 to 44 999	25 5	19 1	4 3	14 8	6 1
$45 000 to 69 999	26 5	21 7	4 0	17 7	4 5
$70 000 and over	25 0	19 0	3 4	15 6	6 0
Family structure					
Two parent family	25 6	20 1	3 7	16 4	5 3
Female parent family	21 4	15 6	3 7	12 0	5 7
Not living with parent	10 9	6 5	3 6	2 9	4 4
While aged 15					
Total	37 6	31 2	6 5	24 7	6 4
Sex					
Male	41 5	34 5	6 1	28 4	6 9
Female	33 5	27 7	7 0	20 6	5 8
Race and Hispanic origin					
White	44 0	37 7	7 5	30 2	6 2
Black	22 2	15 3	2 6	12 7	6 9
Hispanic origin	26 5	20 5	7 7	12 9	5 6
Household income					
Less than $25 000	32 3	26 2	7 4	18 8	6 1
$25 000 to 44 999	40 8	32 5	6 1	26 3	8 1
$45 000 to 69 999	39 8	35 3	6 1	29 2	4 5
$70 000 and over	42 2	35 8	6 6	29 2	6 4
Family structure					
Two parent family	38 6	32 5	5 2	27 3	6 1
Female parent family	38 2	32 5	8 7	23 8	5 5
Not living with parent	25 9	15 9	4 5	11 4	10 1

NOTE The National Longitudinal Survey of Youth 1997 consists of young men and women who were aged 12 to 16 on December 31 1996 Race and Hispanic origin groups are mutually exclusive Totals include American ndians Alaskan Natives and Asians and Pacific slanders not shown sepa rately "While aged 14" refers to the entire year between the individuals 14th and 15th birthdays The first 13 rows exclude individuals who were not yet 15 years of aged when interviewed   "While aged 15" refers to the entire year between the in dividuals 15th and 16th birthdays The last 13 rows exclude individuals who were not yet 16 years of age when interviewed

Tab e 3.3. **Work status during the school year of youths while aged 14 and 15 in 1994-97, by sex, race, Hispanic origin, household income, and family structure**

Age in 1994 97 and characteristic	Did not work	Worked 50 percent of school weeks or fewer		Worked more than 50 percent of school weeks	
		Averaged 14 or fewer hours per week	Averaged 15 or more hours per week	Averaged 14 or fewer hours per week	Averaged 15 or more hours per week
While aged 14					
Total	81 6	3 7	4 7	5 7	3 6
Sex					
Male	77 6	4 5	5 8	6 2	4 9
Female	85 8	2 9	3 5	5 2	2 2
Race and Hispanic origin					
White	77 9	4 3	5 4	7 3	4 3
Black	90 1	1 5	4 0	2 1	1 9
Hispanic origin	88 1	3 3	3 5	2 1	2 0
Household income					
Less than $25 000	84 8	3 1	5 1	2 9	3 4
$25 000 to 44 999	80 9	3 2	5 6	5 4	4 8
$45 000 to 69 999	78 3	3 7	5 5	7 5	3 9
$70 000 and over	81 0	5 0	4 3	6 4	2 8
Family structure					
Two parent family	79 9	3 9	4 8	6 7	4 0
Female parent family	84 4	3 4	4 8	3 7	3 2
Not living with parent	93 5	1 1	3 3	1 1	1 1
While aged 15					
Total	68 8	5 1	9 1	7 3	8 2
Sex					
Male	65 5	4 5	10 0	8 4	9 9
Female	72 3	5 7	8 2	6 2	6 4
Race and Hispanic origin					
White	62 3	6 3	10 5	8 9	10 3
Black	84 7	2 4	6 0	3 2	3 1
Hispanic origin	79 5	3 6	7 8	3 5	3 9
Household income					
Less than $25 000	73 8	4 6	8 2	4 1	7 9
$25 000 to 44 999	67 5	5 0	10 0	5 6	11 2
$45 000 to 69 999	64 7	6 8	7 5	9 4	10 3
$70 000 and over	64 2	6 1	10 3	10 2	7 5
Family structure					
Two parent family	67 5	4 7	8 7	8 6	9 0
Female parent family	67 5	5 9	10 5	6 4	8 5
Not living with parent	84 1	4 1	4 1	3 4	2 3

NOTE The National Longitudinal Survey of Youth 1997 consists of young men and women who were aged 12 to 16 on December 31 1996 Race and Hispanic origin groups are mutually exclusive Totals include American ndians Alaskan Natives and Asians and Pacific slanders not shown sepa rately "While aged 14" refers to the entire year between the individuals 14th and 15th birthdays The first 13 rows exclude individuals who were not yet 15 years of age when interviewed "While aged 15" refers to the entire year between the individu als 15th and 16th birthdays The last 13 rows ex clude individuals who were not yet 16 years of age when interviewed Rows do not add to 100 due to the nonreporting of information on hours and weeks of work for a small number of respondents with employee jobs

Tab e 3.4. **Top 10 industries of longest-held employee job of youths while aged 14 and 15 in 1994-97**

ndustry	Percent
While aged 14	
Eating and drinking places	17 4
Miscellaneous entertainment and recreation services	8 7
Construction	8 4
Newspaper publishing and printing	4 9
Agricultural production crops	4 4
Private households (personal services)	4 1
Landscape and horticultural services	3 6
Agricultural production livestock	2 9
Elementary and secondary schools	1 9
Services to dwellings and other buildings	1 9
While aged 15	
Eating and drinking places	28 8
Miscellaneous entertainment and recreation services	9 0
Construction	5 3
Grocery stores	4 5
Newspaper publishing and printing	2 9
Landscape and horticultural services	2 3
Agricultural production crops	2 0
Agricultural production livestock	1 8
Automotive repair and related services	1 6
Private households (personal services)	1 5

NOTE   The National Longitudinal Survey of Youth 1997 consists of young men and women who were aged 12 to 16 on December 31 1996 "While aged 14" refers to the entire year between the in dividuals 14th and 15th birthdays   The first 10 rows exclude individuals who were not yet 15 years of age when interviewed "While aged 15" refers to the entire year between the individuals 15th and 16th birthdays The last 10 rows exclude individu als who were not yet 16 years of age when inter viewed

Tab e 3.5. **Top 10 industries of longest-held employee job of youths while aged 14 in 1994-97, by sex**

ndustry	Percent
Males	
Eating and drinking places	15 8
Construction	11 4
Miscellaneous entertainment and recreation services	8 8
Newspaper publishing and printing	6 1
Agricultural production crops	5 9
Landscape and horticultural services	5 4
Agricultural production livestock	3 7
Elementary and secondary schools	2 4
Automotive repair and related services	2 3
Grocery stores	1 8
Females	
Eating and drinking places	19 8
Private households (personal services)	8 6
Miscellaneous entertainment and recreation services	8 5
Construction	3 8
Child day care services	3 5
Newspaper publishing and printing	3 1
Religious organizations	2 8
Services to dwellings and other buildings	2 1
Social services not elsewhere classified	1 9
Agricultural production crops	1 9

NOTE   The National Longitudinal Survey of Youth 1997 consists of young men and women who were aged 12 to 16 on December 31 1996 "While aged 14" refers to the entire year between the individuals 14th and 15th birthdays   All rows exclude individuals who were not yet 15 years of age when interviewed

Tab e 3.6. **Top 10 industries of longest-held employee job of youths while aged 15 in 1995-97, by sex**

ndustry	Percent
Males	
Eating and drinking places	27 3
Construction	8 3
Miscellaneous entertainment and recreation services	7 6
Grocery stores	4 7
Newspaper publishing and printing	4 2
Landscape and horticultural services	4 0
Agricultural production crops	2 6
Agricultural production livestock	2 5
Automotive repair and related services	2 0
Miscellaneous retail stores	1 5
Females	
Eating and drinking places	30 8
Miscellaneous entertainment and recreation services	10 9
Grocery stores	4 2
Private households (personal services)	3 0
Religious organizations	2 3
Child day care services	2 3
Services to dwellings and other buildings	1 7
Apparel and accessory stores except shoe	1 6
Food stores not elsewhere classified	1 5
Hotels and motels	1 4

NOTE   The National Longitudinal Survey of Youth 1997 consists of young men and women who were aged 12 to 16 on December 31 1996 "While aged 15" refers to the entire year between the in dividuals 15th and 16th birthdays   All rows ex clude individuals who were not yet 16 years of age when interviewed

Tab e 3.7. **Top 10 occupations of longest-held employee job of youths while aged 14 and 15 in 1994-97**

Occupation	Percent
While aged 14	
Janitors and cleaners	8 7
Farm workers	5 9
Cashiers	5 5
News vendors	5 3
Groundskeepers and gardeners except farm	4 5
Laborers except construction	4 1
Construction laborers	3 9
Cooks	3 8
Waiters and waitresses assistants	3 5
General office clerks	2 9
While aged 15	
Cashiers	10 0
Cooks	5 9
Miscellaneous food preparation occupations	5 7
Janitors and cleaners	5 5
Waiters and waitresses assistants	4 7
Stock handlers and baggers	4 5
Laborers except construction	4 2
Sales workers other commodities	4 1
Construction laborers	3 1
News vendors	3 0

NOTE   The National Longitudinal Survey of Youth 1997 consists of young men and women who were aged 12 to 16 on December 31 1996 "While aged 14" refers to the entire year between the in dividuals 14th and 15th birthdays   The first 10 rows exclude individuals who were not yet 15 years of age when interviewed   "While aged 15" refers to the entire year between the individuals 15th and 16th birthdays   The last 10 rows exclude individu als who were not yet 16 years of age when inter viewed

Tab e 3.8. **Top 10 occupations of longest-held employee job of youths while aged 14 in 1994-97, by sex**

Occupation	Percent
Males	
Janitors and cleaners	9 4
Farm workers	7 1
Groundskeepers and gardeners except farm	6 9
News vendors	6 7
Construction laborers	5 9
Laborers except construction	4 7
Cooks	4 2
Waiters and waitresses assistants	4 1
Miscellaneous food preparation occupations	3 4
Attendants amusement and recreational facilities	2 8
Females	
Cashiers	10 9
Janitors and cleaners	7 5
Child care workers private household	5 9
General office clerks	5 8
Child care workers not elsewhere classified	5 2
Waiters and waitresses	4 7
Receptionists	4 3
Teachers not elsewhere classified	3 9
Farm workers	3 9
Secretaries	3 5

NOTE The National Longitudinal Survey of Youth 1997 consists of young men and women who were aged 12 to 16 on December 31 1996 "While aged 14" refers to the entire year between the individuals 14th and 15th birthdays All rows exclude individuals who were not yet 15 years of age when interviewed

Tab e 3.9. **Top 10 occupations of longest-held employee job of youths while aged 15 in 1995-97, by sex**

Occupation	Percent
Males	
Cooks	7 7
Janitors and cleaners	6 9
Miscellaneous food preparation occupations	6 4
Waiters and waitresses assistants	6 0
Cashiers	5 8
Construction laborers	5 5
Stock handlers and baggers	5 5
Groundskeepers and gardeners except farm	5 1
Laborers except construction	4 8
News vendors	4 5
Females	
Cashiers	15 7
Waiters and waitresses	5 7
General office clerks	5 6
Sales workers other commodities	4 7
Miscellaneous food preparation occupations	4 7
Receptionists	4 1
Cooks	3 6
Janitors and cleaners	3 6
Laborers except construction	3 4
Teachers not elsewhere classified	3 3

NOTE The National Longitudinal Survey of Youth 1997 consists of young men and women who were aged 12 to 16 on December 31 1996 "While aged 15" refers to the entire year between the individuals 15th and 16th birthdays All rows exclude individuals who were not yet 16 years of age when interviewed

Tab e 3.10. **Percent of youths engaged in freelance jobs while aged 14 and 15 in 1994-97, by type of job, sex, race, Hispanic origin, and household income**

Age in 1994 97 and characteristic	Percent with a freelance job	Percent of those with a freelance job engaged in	
		Babysitting	Yard work
While aged 14			
Total	42 8	62 0	37 9
Sex			
Male	36 8	24 6	72 8
Female	49 1	91 4	10 6
Race and Hispanic origin			
White	48 3	63 3	37 4
Black	33 1	55 2	41 1
Hispanic origin	30 1	59 9	40 2
Household income			
Less than $25 000	34 7	58 7	35 1
$25 000 to 44 999	46 4	63 2	39 1
$45 000 to 69 999	49 3	61 5	41 1
$70 000 and over	49 5	67 8	35 0
While aged 15			
Total	39 8	59 8	37 2
Sex			
Male	34 1	19 6	72 8
Female	45 8	91 4	9 3
Race and Hispanic origin			
White	44 8	61 0	37 2
Black	28 7	52 9	41 2
Hispanic origin	28 1	59 7	34 1
Household income			
Less than $25 000	30 9	52 3	33 0
$25 000 to 44 999	44 7	64 3	33 6
$45 000 to 69 999	46 9	61 1	42 8
$70 000 and over	49 4	62 3	39 5

NOTE   The National Longitudinal Survey of Youth 1997 consists of young men and women who were aged 12 to 16 on December 31 1996 Race and Hispanic origin groups are mutually exclusive Totals include American ndians Alaskan Natives and Asians and Pacific slanders not shown sepa rately   "While aged 14" refers to the entire year between the individuals 14th and 15th birthdays The first 10 rows exclude individuals who were not yet 15 years of age when interviewed   "While aged 15" refers to the entire year between the individu als 15th and 16th birthdays   The last 10 rows ex clude individuals who were not yet 16 years of age when interviewed

Tab e 3.11. **Percent of youths engaged in work activities while aged 12 in 1995-97, by type of job, sex, race, Hispanic origin, and household income**

Age in 1995 97 and characteristic	Percent with a work activity	Percent of those with a work activity engaged in	
		Babysitting	Yard work
Total while aged 12	49 6	55 6	39 7
Sex			
Male	48 3	26 3	65 8
Female	51 0	84 9	13 6
Race and Hispanic origin			
White	56 5	54 6	40 1
Black	36 2	46 9	41 7
Hispanic origin	36 0	61 3	37 0
Household income			
Less than $25 000	48 7	50 1	45 9
$25 000 to 44 999	52 2	51 2	41 5
$45 000 to 69 999	53 8	55 6	39 1
$70 000 and over	53 9	61 5	39 1

NOTE   The National Longitudinal Survey of Youth 1997 consists of young men and women who were aged 12 to 16 on December 31 1996   Race and Hispanic origin groups are mutually exclusive   Totals include American ndians Alaskan Natives and Asians and Pacific slanders not shown sepa rately   "While aged 12" refers to the entire year between the individuals 12th and 13th birthdays   All rows exclude individuals who were not yet 13 years of age when interviewed

Tab e 3.12. **Percent of youths in 9th or higher grades in 1997 who participated in school-to-work programs, by sex, race, Hispanic origin, and household income**

Characteristic	Any program	Job shadowing	Mentoring	Coopera tive education	School sponsored enterprise	Technical prepara tion	nternship or appren ticeship	Career major
Total	38 8	12 6	4 8	6 8	9 1	7 6	4 3	18 3
Sex								
Male	38 6	11 0	4 6	7 3	8 9	8 5	4 3	19 1
Female	39 0	14 2	5 0	6 3	9 3	6 6	4 3	17 4
Race and Hispanic origin								
White	38 5	13 5	4 1	6 3	9 0	7 0	3 9	17 3
Black	46 0	11 5	6 7	10 3	10 5	10 5	6 6	24 8
Hispanic origin	32 1	9 0	4 7	5 4	7 2	6 9	4 1	15 9
Household income								
Less than $25 000	39 5	11 2	4 1	8 4	7 8	7 7	5 9	19 9
$25 000 to 44 999	41 5	12 5	5 7	6 9	10 1	8 3	3 7	19 7
$45 000 to 69 999	39 6	13 8	5 5	6 0	10 2	8 8	3 6	18 6
$70 000 and over	38 9	14 8	4 2	5 9	9 5	6 2	4 1	15 0

NOTE   The National Longitudinal Survey of Youth 1997 consists of young men and women who were aged 12 to 16 on December 31 1996   Race and Hispanic origin groups are mutually exclusive   Totals include American ndians Alaskan Natives and Asians and Pacific slanders not shown separately

Chapter 4.
Trends in Youth Employment: Data from the Current Population Survey

Introduction

This chapter provides a look at trends in the employment of youths aged 15 to 17 from the Current Population Survey (CPS), a monthly labor force survey of 50,000 households. Each month, interviewed households are asked a series of questions to determine employment status and other employment-related information about all persons aged 15 or older during the week of the 12th. CPS data normally are published only for the population aged 16 and older. For this special report on youths, data for 15-year-olds were tabulated to provide new knowledge on youth employment patterns.

Like the preceding chapter, which used data from the National Longitudinal Survey of Youth 1997 (NLSY97), this chapter presents data from the CPS on incidence and type of employment for youths in various demographic and income groups. It also provides information on youth unemployment, hours of work, and earnings, and examines differences between youths enrolled in school and dropouts. Unlike the previous chapter, this chapter focuses on trends, as the CPS is the only BLS survey that provides information on youth employment over many years. Differences between the NLSY97 and the CPS are discussed in detail in the appendix at the end of this chapter.

Time frames for comparison

This chapter looks at employment during the 1978-98 period. Through much of this chapter, data were pooled across several years in order to bolster the sample sizes and thereby improve the reliability of estimates.[1] In most sections, data are described in 3-year combinations reflecting the periods 1977-79, 1987-89, and 1996-98. The periods for the pooled data were selected because they reflect similar points in the business cycle: they all occur well into economic expansions. Thus, fluctuations in youth employment from period to period that might have been attributable to business cycle changes are minimized. For some analyses, annual average data are used to show trends over time. Other portions of the discussion rely on monthly data from special supplements to the CPS.

Because youth employment is much more common in the summer than in school months, averages of weekly youth employment figures are analyzed for school months and summer months separately, whenever possible. The CPS permits school-month versus summer-month comparisons in nearly all cases. Annual averages are presented only when school and summer months show similar patterns.[2] Unless otherwise specified, data in the text refer to the school months of the 1996-98 period.

How many youths work?

Employment. During the 1996-98 period, 2.9 million youths aged 15 to 17 worked during school months, and 4.0 million worked during the summer months.[3] Each month, the CPS determines the employment status of youths (and other workers) by determining whether they worked for pay or had a job from which they were temporarily absent in the week prior to the week during which they were interviewed. These data are gathered for all persons aged 15 and older through personal interviews and computer-assisted telephone interviews.[4] Those who worked for pay at least 1 hour during the reference week, and those who worked for no pay in a family business for at least 15 hours, are considered employed.

Among youths, employment increased markedly with age. During the school months of 1996-98, the CPS found that only 9 percent of 15-year-olds were employed in an average month, compared with 26 percent of those a year older and 39 percent of 17-year-olds. Youths in each age group were more likely to work in the summer, during which employment rates increased to 18, 36, and 48 percent at each age, respectively. The very low rates for 15-year-olds in part reflect legal restrictions on the types and hours of employment allowed for persons under age 16. (See chapter 2 on legal issues.)

The CPS showed that male and female youths had similar employment-population ratios. In 1996-98, about a fourth of both male and female youths were employed during average school months. During the summer, about a third of both male and female youths worked. (See table 4.1.) There were substantial differences in employment rates across race/ethnicity groups.[5] The 1996-98 employment-population ratio of white youths—28 percent during the school months and 38 percent during the summer—was about twice that of black (13 and 20 percent) and

Hispanic (15 and 20 percent) youths. This pattern has persisted for many years.

Despite popular perceptions that youths work more than they did in the past, the proportion of 15- to 17-year-olds who work has declined over time. As shown in chart 4.1, employment-population ratios declined with economic downturns in the early 1980s and 1990s. After the decline in the early 1990s, however, the rates did not return to earlier levels. During the most recent 3-year period, 1996-98, a quarter of youths worked during the school months, down from 30 percent in 1977-79. Just over a third worked during the summer, down from 43 percent during the late 1970s.

Additionally, the potential pool of young workers declined over the period. In 1977-79, the population of youths aged 15 to 17 totaled 12.4 million. That level fell during the 1980s, as the last members of the baby-boom generation moved into their twenties. The number of youths rose again during the mid- and late-1990s; in 1996-98, there were about 11.7 million youths aged 15 to 17. The combination of the declines in the youth population and declines in the proportion working led to reductions in the overall number of youths with jobs. The 2.9 million employed youths in the school months of 1996-98 represented a 28-percent decline from 1977-79.

Employment-population ratios fell among youths at each age, but the drop was largest among 15-year-olds. The proportion of 15-year-olds who worked fell from 30 to 18 percent during the summer months and from 17 to 9 percent during the school year. Employment declined for workers of both sexes, but the drop was more pronounced among male youths. As a result, employment-population ratios that had been higher for male than for female youths in 1977-79 were about the same as those for female youths in the 1996-98 period. Employment also declined between 1977-79 and 1996-98 for white and Hispanic youths. Black youths' employment-population ratios, by comparison, were down only

slightly during the summer months, and actually increased during the school year.

Unemployment. The CPS provides information on jobseeking by youths as well as their employment. In the CPS, persons are identified as "unemployed" if they: 1) did not work during the reference week (the week before the survey), 2) were available to work that week, and 3) had actively sought work during the past 4 weeks. Youths who were not employed during the week and also did not fit all of the above criteria are classified as out of the labor force. In the summer months of 1996-98, an average of 2.9 million youths aged 15 to 17 were employed and 665,000 were unemployed. By far the largest group—8.2 million—was out of the labor force.

Unemployment rates equal the number of unemployed persons as a percent of the labor force (the employed plus unemployed), and are typically used as indicators of labor market difficulty of various groups. Those persons who are out of the labor force are not included in the calculation.

Youth unemployment rates are much higher than the rates for other groups. Combining summer and school months, the annual average unemployment rate of 15- to 17-year-olds in 1996-98 was 19 percent. That compared with 14 percent for persons aged 18 and 19, and 4 percent for those aged 20 and older. The higher rates for youths may reflect the limited range of jobs available to persons with the least experience in the labor market and the most limited job skills. They also reflect the more transitory nature of youth employment. For example, some youths work at summer jobs, but stop working or seek a different employment arrangement during the school year. These transitions mean that they might be seeking work more frequently than are others and, hence, be identified as unemployed. Others might be exploring their interests or complementing a school schedule. As a result, youths often have repeated spells of unemployment during

the year and are, therefore, more likely to be counted among the unemployed in any month.

Unemployment rates among youths are about the same during the school and summer months. In 1996-98, male youths were slightly more likely than female youths to be unemployed — 20 versus 17 percent (in both school and summer months). Rates declined with age. In the school months of 1996-98, the unemployment rate was 24 percent for 15-year-olds; it fell to 21 percent among 16-year-olds and to 16 percent among 17-year-olds. (See table 4.2.)

As shown in chart 4.2, black and Hispanic youths had much higher unemployment rates than did white youths. During the school months of 1996–98, 35 percent of black youths and 30 percent of Hispanic youths aged 15 to 17 were unemployed, compared with 17 percent of whites.

Over the 1977-98 period, unemployment fluctuated, increasing during economic downturns and declining during expansions. When analysis is limited to the three expansionary periods to reduce the effect of business cycles, table 4.2 shows that school-month unemployment rates were about unchanged for male youths between the 1977-79 and 1996-98 periods, while they were down slightly for female youths. While rates for white and Hispanic youths were relatively stable over the period, the unemployment rate for blacks dropped from 44 to 35 percent. The estimates for summer months showed a similar pattern.

Factors affecting youth employment and unemployment

Employment-population ratios and unemployment rates of youths vary by characteristics such as family income and type, school enrollment status, and country of origin. These factors are discussed below.

Family income. Each year, the March supplement to the Current Population Survey includes questions on total family income. Table 4.3 includes the

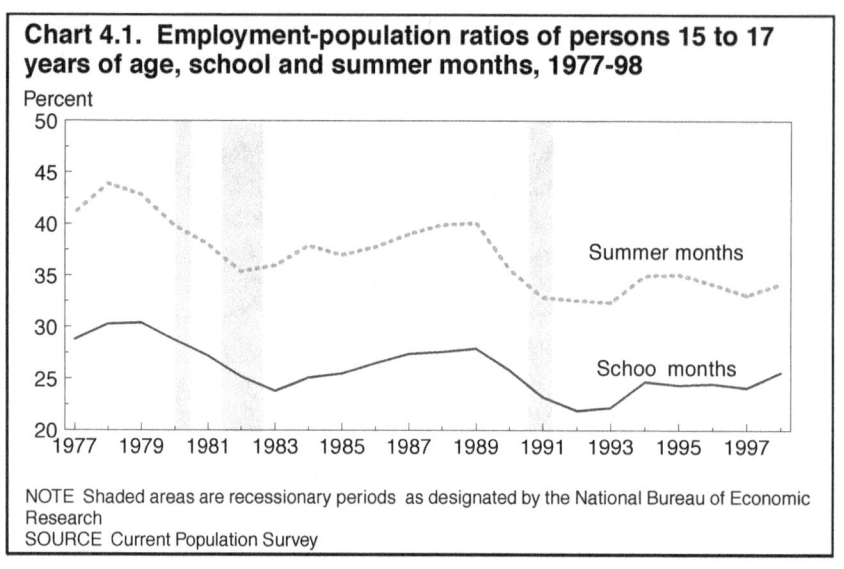

Chart 4.1. Employment-population ratios of persons 15 to 17 years of age, school and summer months, 1977-98

Percent

Summer months

Schoo months

NOTE Shaded areas are recessionary periods as designated by the National Bureau of Economic Research

SOURCE Current Population Survey

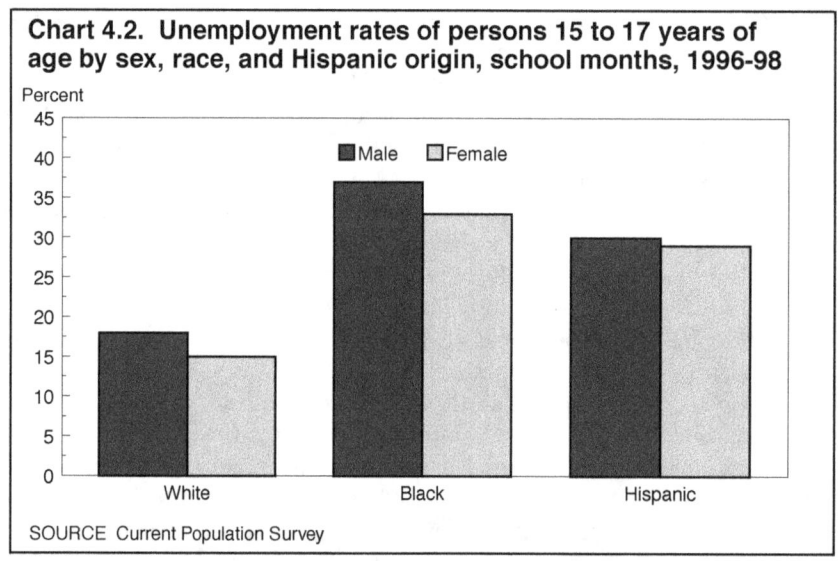

Chart 4.2. Unemployment rates of persons 15 to 17 years of age by sex, race, and Hispanic origin, school months, 1996-98

Percent

■ Male □ Female

White   Black   Hispanic

SOURCE Current Population Survey

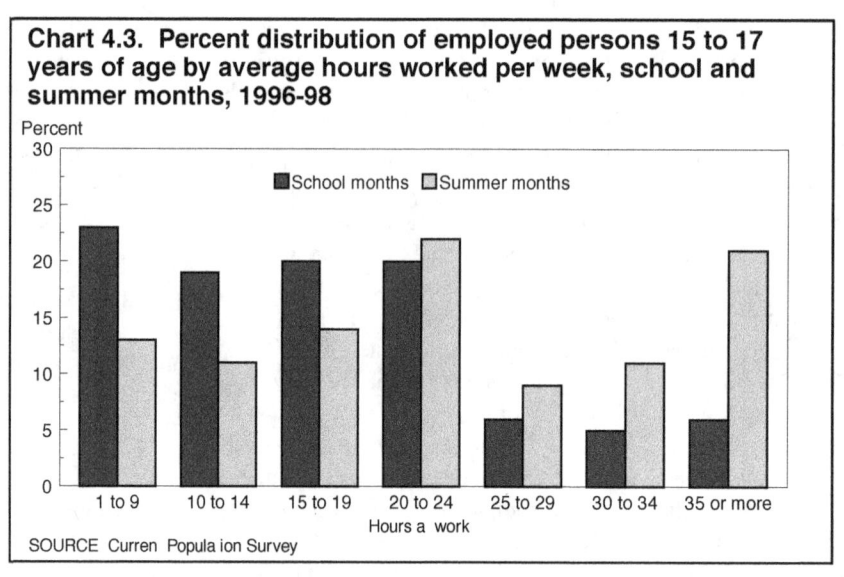

Chart 4.3. Percent distribution of employed persons 15 to 17 years of age by average hours worked per week, school and summer months, 1996-98

Percent

■ School months □ Summer months

1 to 9   10 to 14   15 to 19   20 to 24   25 to 29   30 to 34   35 or more

Hours a work

SOURCE Curren Popula ion Survey

data from the March 1999 supplement, showing employment status during March 1999 and family income by quartile in 1998.[6] Like the NLSY97 data, CPS data show that youths in higher-income families are more likely to work than are those in lower-income families.

Only 15 percent of youths whose families had incomes in the lowest quartile of the distribution were employed in March 1999. The employment-population ratio rose to 22 percent among those in the second quartile and to 30 percent in the third and fourth family income groups. A similar pattern emerged within each race/ethnicity group; however, not all differences between income groups were statistically significant, as small samples for some race/ethnicity groups within income groups resulted in wide variances on the estimates.

Unemployment rates among youths decline as family income increases. In March 1999, 31 percent of youths who were in the labor force and from families in the lowest income quartile (in 1998) were unemployed. By contrast, only 12 percent of those whose families had incomes in the top quarter of the distribution were unemployed. Data for March 1990 and March 1980 (family income in 1989 and 1979, respectively) also are shown in table 4.3, and suggest that these patterns in employment and unemployment have existed for many years.

Family type. Youths in married-couple families and those not living with relatives were more likely to be employed than were those in single-parent families. (See above tabulation.) In the school months of 1996-98, 27 percent of youths in married-couple families and 29 percent of those living alone held a job, compared with 19 and 23 percent of those in families maintained by an unmarried woman or man. The unemployment rate for youths in married-couple families was the lowest among the groups—15 percent, compared with 29 percent for those in families maintained by women and 23 percent in families

Employment status of persons 15 to 17 years of age by family type, school months, 1996-98

Measure	Total	In married-couple families	In families maintained by women	In families maintained by men	Not living with relatives
Employment-population ratio...	24.7	26.7	19.1	22.9	28.6
Unemployment rate.................	18.7	15.0	29.1	23.1	—

Dash indicates data not shown where base is less than 50,000.

maintained by men.

As mentioned in chapter 3, families with more adults are generally more affluent than are those with fewer adults. Youths in families with more adults or higher incomes may have greater access to a car or to an adult who will drive them to a place of work. It may also be easier for youths from higher-income families to find employment. Youths in more affluent communities may also benefit from relatively tight local labor markets.

It is also possible that nonmarket work, such as housework and unpaid child care, more often falls to youths in single-parent families than to those in married-couple families. This would make youths in single-parent families relatively less available for market work—or available only for specific schedules. Their higher unemployment rates indicate, however, that even among those who are available to work, youths in those families are less successful at finding employment.

School enrollment status. Each October, the CPS includes supplementary questions on the school enrollment status of members of the household. From this supplement, it is possible to

look at the employment patterns of youths enrolled in high school compared with the patterns of those who dropped out between the October when they were surveyed and the previous October. Table 4.4 shows that the influence of dropping out of high school affects employment differently for male and female youths. In October 1996–98, male dropouts were much more likely to work than were those who were still in school—40 versus 26 percent, respectively. Female dropouts, by contrast, were about as likely to work as were their enrolled counterparts. This probably reflects different reasons for dropping out by gender. Female dropouts often leave school to have a child; caring for the child restricts their labor force availability.[7] Race comparisons were not possible, as there were too few black high school dropouts (48,000) to produce reliable estimates. Employment-population ratios for the three expansionary periods in this study indicate that employment was down both among youths enrolled in high school and among dropouts.

Unemployment was higher for high school dropouts than for those enrolled in school. (See tabulation below.) Sample sizes are large enough to compare some selected subgroups of

Unemployment rates of persons 15 to 17 years of age by school enrollment status, October 1996-98

Group	Number of high school dropouts (in thousands)	Unemployment rate, high school dropouts	Unemployment rate, youths enrolled in high school
Total, 15 to 17 years	281	31.6	15.8
Male	138	29.9	16.8
Female	143	34.3	14.7
White	220	27.5	13.9
Total, age 17	183	31.2	12.6

youths.[8] As shown, dropouts' overall unemployment rate is nearly twice that of youths still enrolled in school, and substantially higher rates occur among dropouts than among enrollees for all the groups shown.

Country of birth. As was found in the NLSY97, the CPS also showed that youths who were not born in the United States were less likely to be employed than were those born in the United States. Of the 15- to 17-year-old foreign-born youths, 15 percent were working when surveyed in 1994-98, compared with 28 percent of U.S.-born youths.[9] Unemployment rates also were substantially higher for foreign-born youths: 27 percent, versus 19 percent for those born in the United States. As mentioned in chapter 3, these patterns may reflect a combination of factors that could reduce the relative success of foreign-born youths at finding employment, such as problems speaking English, lower relative job search skills, fewer employment contacts, or employment discrimination.[10]

How much do youths work?

One strength of the CPS is that it collects information on hours worked per week. CPS respondents are asked to report the total hours they actually worked during the week prior to the survey. Employed youths work fewer hours per week during the school months than during the summer. (See table 4.5.) In 1996-98, employed youths (who were at work during the survey week) aged 15 to 17 worked an average of about 17 hours a week during the school months and 23 hours during the summer months.

Like employment, average hours worked increased with age. During the school months of 1996-98, employed 15-year-olds worked 12 hours per week, 16-year-olds worked 16 hours, and 17-year-olds worked 18 hours. The summer-month figures were 19, 23, and 25 hours, respectively. In 1996-98, employed male

Average hours at work per week of persons 15 to 17 years of age by country of birth, 1994–98

Group	Number of employed foreign-born youths (in thousands)	Average hours, foreign-born youths	Average hours, youths born in the United States
Total, 15 to 17 years	108	23.8	18.2
Male	63	25.8	19.1
White	73	25.5	18.1
Hispanic	56	27.8	20.4
Total, age 17	64	25.1	19.9

youths worked more hours than did female youths in both the school and summer months. White youths were most likely to hold jobs, but employed Hispanic youths worked the most hours per week—21 hours during the school months, compared with 16 hours for white youths and 18 hours for black youths.

High school dropouts worked many more hours than did those enrolled in high school. In 1996-98, employed dropouts worked an average of 34 hours per week, while those enrolled in school worked 15 hours per week. The number of employed dropouts is not large enough to make comparisons by age, sex, or race. Employed youths born outside the United States work more hours than do their U.S.-born peers. As shown in the tabulation above, in 1994-98, foreign-born youths worked an average of 24 hours, compared with 18 hours worked by those

born in the United States. Differences persist across groups for which a comparison could be made.

Chart 4.3 shows a distribution of weekly work hours among youths during the summer and school months. During the school year, many employed youths worked a small number of hours. About 25 percent of employed youths worked 9 or fewer hours during the school months, compared with 13 percent during the summer. Only 6 percent of employed youths worked full-time (35 hours or more per week) during the school year, compared with 20 percent during the summer.

Over time, the average number of hours worked by youths fell during the summer months; hours worked during the school months were relatively flat. Chart 4.4 shows annual average hours trends for employed youths (at work) aged 15 to 17. Hours dropped sub-

Chart 4.4. Average hours at work of persons 15 to 17 years of age, school and summer months, 1977-98

NOTE: Shaded areas are recessionary periods as designated by the National Bureau of Economic Research

SOURCE: Current Population Survey

Hourly earnings of persons 15 to 17 years of age, 1998

Age	Tota pa d by the hour (n thousands)	Percent pa d:		
		Be ow the m n mum wage	At the m n mum wage	Above the m n mum wage
Tota , 15 to 17 years	2,908	17	12	71
15 years	353	27	14	59
16 years	980	17	13	71
17 years	1,574	15	11	74

stantially in the late 1970s and during the downturns of the early 1980s. They climbed a bit in the expansionary period in the 1980s but did not return to 1970s levels. Hours dropped again during the subsequent downturn in the early 1990s. Hours of work during school months returned to prerecession levels, but summer months did not.

Table 4.5 compares the specified 3-year periods to minimize the influence of business cycle fluctuations. As shown, average hours during the school year were relatively flat at about 17 percent in each period, while summer-month work hours dropped from 27 to 23 hours between the 1977-79 and 1996-98 periods. Male youths worked more hours than did female youths in both the school and summer months in all three periods. The pattern of longer work hours for Hispanic youths than for white or black youths also persisted in the school months of all three periods studied.

How much do youths earn?

The minimum wage often is associated with young workers first entering the labor force. CPS data indicate that earnings were above the minimum wage for most youths. The minimum was $5.15 in 1998.[11] The CPS measures hourly earnings of wage and salary workers paid hourly rates. Of the 3.3 million youths employed in 1998, 2.9 million (89 percent) were included in this hourly pay calculation.

Hourly earnings in the school and summer months are about the same. Thus, annual averages are used for comparisons in this section. In 1998, median earnings of 15- to 17-year-olds combined were $5.57 per hour. In 1998, hourly earnings increased with age: 15-year-olds earned a median of $5.38 per hour, 16-year-olds earned $5.52, and 17-year-olds earned $5.65 per hour. Earnings varied slightly across sex and race groups. Hispanic and white males had the highest median hourly earnings; Hispanic and black females had the lowest. (See

table 4.6.) Chart 4.5 shows the earnings distribution of youths by single year of age. As shown, the vast majority of workers at each age have earnings between $5 and $7 an hour.

Even among 15-year-olds, most young workers earned more than the 1998 minimum wage of $5.15. As shown in the tabulation above, more than half of 15-year-olds earned more than the minimum wage. A quarter earned less than the minimum wage, as some occupations—including many food service jobs—are exempt from the minimum wage or may pay a training wage for a specified period. The proportion of employed youths who earned more than the minimum wage increased to 71 percent of 16-year-olds and to three-fourths of those aged 17.

Earnings of youths in 1998 were lower in real terms than in 1979 and higher than in 1989.[12] The Federal minimum wage in force in 1989 was set in 1981, and the minimum was not raised until 1990.[13] Over that period,

earnings of youths declined in real terms.

Where do youths work?

In a similar fashion to chapter 3, the following section examines the types of work youths perform. Data are again pooled across 3-year periods from 1977-79, 1987-89, and 1996-98 and are reported separately for school and summer months. Class of worker, industry, and occupation distributions of employed youth are examined.

Class of worker. In 1996-98, 97 percent of employed youths aged 15 to 17 were classified in the CPS as wage and salary workers. Only 2 percent of the 2.9 million youths aged 15 to 17 working in the school months of the period were self-employed, and fewer than 1 percent were classified as unpaid family workers. (See table 4.7.)

Persons who work for profit or fees in their own business, shop, or farm are classified as self-employed in the

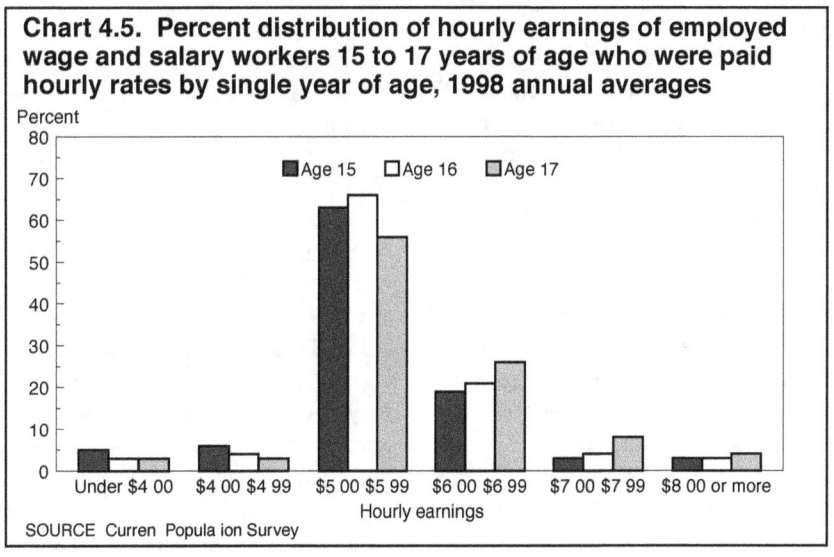

Chart 4.5. Percent distribution of hourly earnings of employed wage and salary workers 15 to 17 years of age who were paid hourly rates by single year of age, 1998 annual averages

SOURCE Curren Popula ion Survey

CPS. Work on an odd-job or casual basis is typically reported as work for a private company, business, or individual. In general, persons who work in another person's home, such as groundskeepers and gardeners or child care providers, are reported in the CPS as wage and salary employees—that is, they work for a private employer. Such persons are not self-employed unless they own a business that provides such services.

Male youths were more likely to be self-employed than were female youths—3 percent versus 2 percent, respectively—in the school months of the 1996-98 period. Self-employment declined with age: about 6 percent of working 15-year-olds were self-employed, compared with only 2 percent of 16-year-olds and 1 percent of 17-year-olds. Self-employment increased in the summer months, particularly in agricultural industries and among male youths, although such work still accounted for only a fraction of all work by youths, and was mostly lawn care.

While reported as self-employed, most such youths fell into jobs traditionally held by young persons: lawn care (groundskeepers and gardeners—22 percent of employed youths in the school months of the 1996-98 period), babysitting (family child care providers—19 percent), and newspaper delivery (news vendors—12 percent). Not surprisingly, a large proportion of self-employed male youths performed lawn care—34 percent in the school months and 64 percent in the summer months. More than 2 in 5 self-employed female youths were employed in family child care—47 percent in school months and 43 percent in summer months.

Fewer than 1 percent of all employed youths in the school months of 1996-98 were unpaid family workers, that is, persons working more than 15 hours per week in a family-owned business. Unpaid family work was more common in agriculture than in nonagricultural industries. In the school months of 1996-98, 9 percent of youths 15 to 17 years of age who were employed in agriculture worked

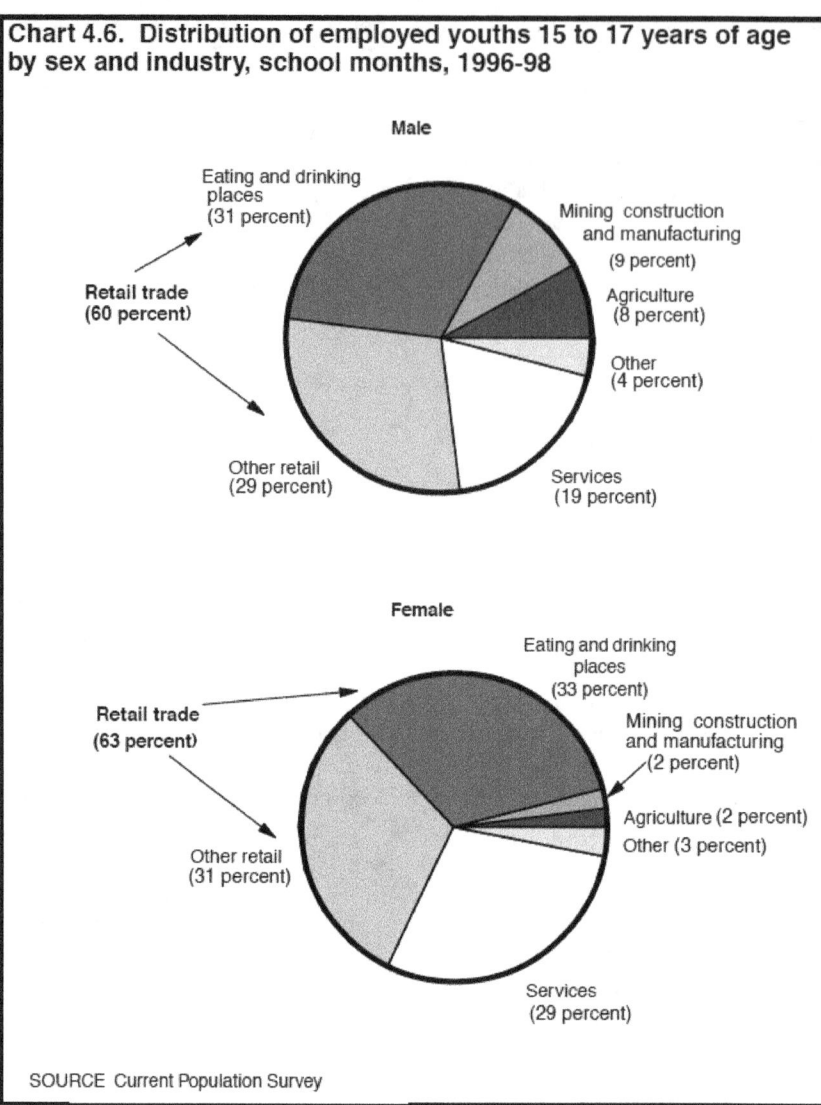

Chart 4.6. Distribution of employed youths 15 to 17 years of age by sex and industry, school months, 1996-98

Male

Eating and drinking places (31 percent)

Mining construction and manufacturing (9 percent)

Agriculture (8 percent)

Retail trade (60 percent)

Other (4 percent)

Other retail (29 percent)

Services (19 percent)

Female

Eating and drinking places (33 percent)

Retail trade (63 percent)

Mining construction and manufacturing (2 percent)

Agriculture (2 percent)

Other (3 percent)

Other retail (31 percent)

Services (29 percent)

SOURCE Current Population Survey

for no pay on a family farm. The percentage of employed youths who were unpaid family workers fell from the 1977-79 period, when 2 percent of all employed youths and 27 percent of youths employed in agriculture were unpaid family workers.

Industry. About 62 percent of youths aged 15 to 17 employed during the school months of the 1996-98 period worked in retail trade, more than in any other major industry. Within retail trade, eating and drinking places accounted for the greatest share of employed youths, about one-third of all employed 15- to 17-year-olds. Another 1 in 4 youths was employed in service industries. In the summer, youth employment was less concen-

trated in retail trade and youths were employed in a wider variety of industries than during the school months. Retail trade still accounted for about half, services increased to 30 percent, and employment in agriculture and goods-producing industries (mining, construction, and manufacturing) increased. This seasonal pattern of employment also was present in earlier periods.

The concentration of youth employment in retail trade increased from 48 percent in the 1977-79 period to 59 percent in 1987-89 and to 62 percent in 1996-98. The share of youths employed in eating and drinking places also increased. The percent of youths employed in services fell from the 1977-79 to 1996-98 period, largely because employment in private households fell from 12 to 3 percent of employed youths. The proportion of youths employed in entertainment and recreation services doubled from 3 to 6 percent of employed youths (from 4 to 9 percent in the summer months). (See table 4.8.)

Male youths were far more likely to work in agriculture (8 percent) and goods-producing industries such as mining, construction, and manufacturing (9 percent combined) than were female youths (2 percent each). Female youths were more likely to work in retail trade (63 percent) and services (29 percent) than their male counterparts (60 and 19 percent, respectively) and also were more likely to be employed in private households (6 percent) than were male youths (1 percent). (See chart 4.6.)

Table 4.9 lists the top 10 industries in which male and female youths worked in the school months of the 1996-98 period. Four of the ten most common detailed industries in which employed male youths worked and six of the top ten industries in which female youths worked were in retail trade. Eating and drinking places and grocery stores were the largest employers of both male youths (accounting for 31 and 14 percent, respectively) and female youths (33 and 10 percent).

Black youths were more likely to be employed in retail trade (71 percent) than were white or Hispanic youths (61 and 62 percent, respectively). Black youths were less likely to be employed in goods-producing industries (3 percent) than were white or Hispanic youths (6 and 8 percent, respectively). White youths were more likely to be employed in agriculture and private households than were their black or Hispanic counterparts.

The percentage of youths employed in retail trade increased between ages 15 and 16, and was driven by increases in the proportion of youths employed in eating and drinking places. The 15-year-olds were more likely to work in agriculture (male youths) and private household services (female youths) than were older employed youths. Re-

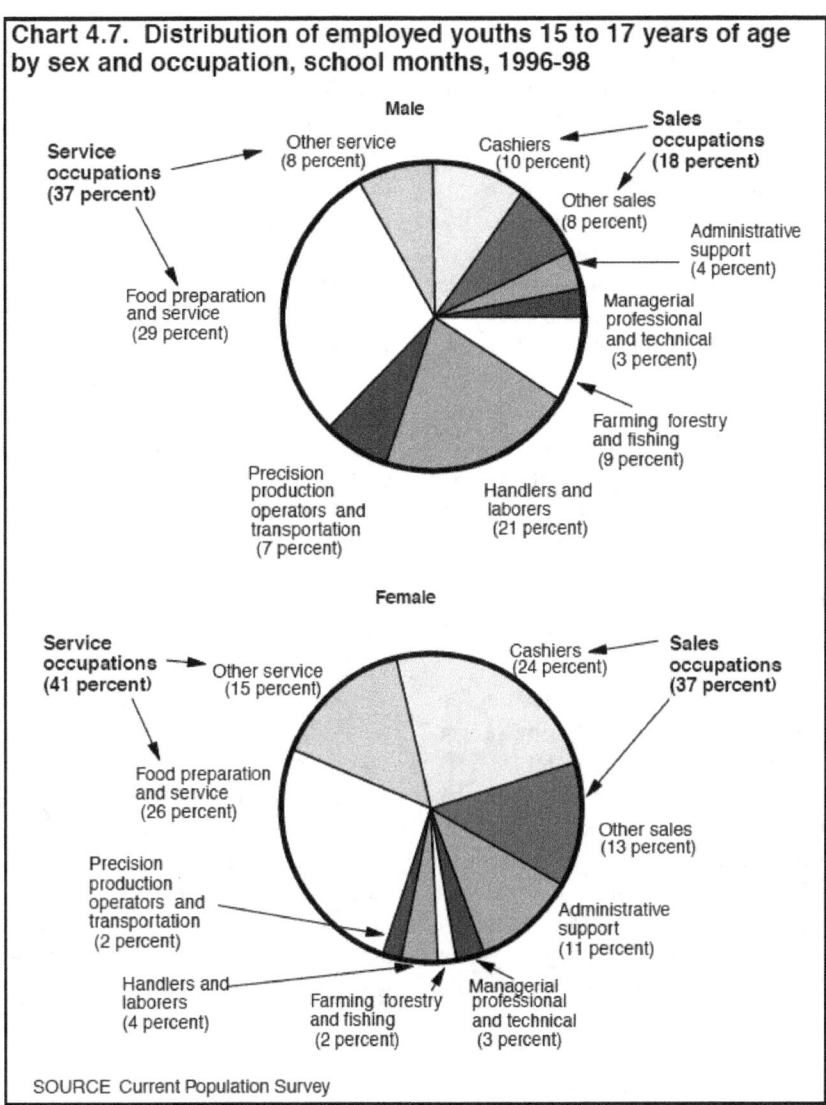

Chart 4.7. Distribution of employed youths 15 to 17 years of age by sex and occupation, school months, 1996-98

SOURCE Current Population Survey

strictions on types of work available to younger youths, a greater desire for more casual employment arrangements, and legal driving ages that restrict the mobility of 15-year-olds may be responsible for these differences.

Occupation. Occupational data provide a slightly different perspective on youth employment patterns. In the 1996-98 school months, 39 percent of employed youths worked in service occupations and 27 percent worked in sales. Twenty seven percent of working youths were employed in food preparation and service occupations. Thirteen percent of youths were employed in general labor occupations (handlers, equipment cleaners, helpers, and laborers) and 8 percent were

in administrative, including clerical, occupations. In the summer months, more youths were employed in farming occupations and fewer were in sales. (See table 4.10.)

Between the 1987-89 and 1996-98 periods, employment in sales occupations increased slightly from 24 percent to 27 percent.[14] The proportion of youths working as cashiers rose from 12 percent to 17 percent. Employment in services fell slightly from 1987-89 to 1996-98. Within services, a smaller proportion of youths performed child care, but employment in food preparation and service increased. Youth employment in other skilled (precision production occupations, operators, and transportation occupations) and general labor trades decreased over the period.

Male and female youths were about equally likely to work in food preparation and service occupations (29 and 26 percent, respectively). Much larger percentages of male youths were employed in production (7 percent), general labor (21 percent), and farm (9 percent) occupations than was the case for female youths (2, 4, and 2 percent, respectively). Female youths were more likely to be employed in sales occupations (37 percent), particularly as cashiers (24 percent), than were male youths (18 and 10 percent, respectively). Female youths also were more likely to work in administrative support occupations (11 percent) and in child care (7 percent) than were male youths (4 and 1 percent, respectively). (See chart 4.7.)

Table 4.11 shows employment in the 10 largest occupations by gender for the school months of the 1996-98 period. Stock handlers and baggers (13 percent of all working 15- to 17-year-old male youths) and cooks (12 percent) topped the list of occupations among male youths. About 1 of 4 working female youths was a cashier. In the summer months more male

youths worked as landscapers and gardeners and more female youths worked as child care providers.

A larger percentage of black youths were employed in sales (38 percent) than was the case for white or Hispanic youths (26 and 27 percent, respectively). White youths were more likely to provide child care than were black or Hispanic youths. More white youths (6 percent) were employed in farm occupations (primarily as groundskeepers and gardeners) than was the case for Hispanic (4 percent) or black (1 percent) youths.

As noted in chapter 3 and in the industry discussion earlier in this chapter, youths moved out of more casual employment relationships into more formal arrangements as they aged. One in five female youths worked in private household occupations at age 15, but only 5 percent of 16-year-olds and 3 percent of 17-year-olds did so. Among male youths, 18 percent of working 15-year-olds held farming occupations (primarily lawn care). That share fell to 9 percent among 16-year-olds, and 7 percent among 17-year-olds. Older youths were more likely to work in food

preparation and service and administrative support occupations than were younger youths. Only 19 percent of working 15-year-olds held sales jobs, compared with 28 percent of 16-year-olds and 29 percent of 17-year-olds. A larger percentage of 17-year-olds worked in skilled trade occupations than was the case for their younger counterparts.

Summary

Current Population Survey data show that employment and unemployment patterns among 15- to 17-year-olds vary by demographic characteristics such as age, sex, race, and Hispanic origin. Over the 1977-98 period, the proportion of youths holding a job and their hours of work have declined.

The likelihood of youths working or being unemployed is influenced by many factors, including age, race, family type, family income, school-enrollment status, and country of birth. Youths are employed in a variety of occupations and industries, moving out of more casual employment arrangements—such as babysitting and lawn care—to more formal employment arrangements as they get older.

This chapter was contributed by Diane Herz and Karen Kosanovich, economists with the Bureau of Labor Statistics, U.S. Department of Labor. The authors thank Martha Duff, Yen-chun Kuo, Robert McIntire, Patricia Merritt, Josephyne Price, and Edwin Robison for their assistance in the preparation of data for this report.

[1] In an average month in 1998, data were collected for 5,500 youths aged 15, 16, and 17, split about evenly among the three ages. The sample included 4,515 whites, 671 blacks, and 611 Hispanics. Dividing the data into employment status and occupational and industry categories reduces the accuracy of the estimates. When 3 years of data are pooled, variances on estimates of levels and changes are reduced by about two-thirds.

[2] The actual dates when youths attend school and take summer vacations vary across States and some local areas. For this analysis, approximate months of attendance were chosen. School months in a particular year refer to a combination of data from January through May and from September to December of the calendar year. Summer months are defined as June through August.

[3] The employment-population ratio is shown here, rather than the commonly presented labor force participation rate. This choice was made because the components of the labor force—employment and unemployment—vary widely for youths. They are discussed separately. The CPS employment measure is an *average* of employment during each of the 3 summer months or the 9 school months; it is not a measure of work at *any time* across the 3-month or 9-month period (as is the NLSY97 measure of employment during one's 14th or 15th year).

[4] Unlike the NSLY97, which interviews youths about their own employment experience, the CPS allows proxy responses. In fact, household members other than the youths were the primary respondents in 92 percent of households with youths aged 15 to 17. The proportion of households with such proxy response declines as the young person's age increases. In 1998, other members were primary respondents in 94 percent of households with 15-year-olds. The rates were 92 percent and 90 percent in households with 16- and 17-year-olds, respectively. More discussion on the effect of proxy responses on employment estimates is available in the CPS-NLSY comparison in the appendix.

[5] Detail for the white, black, and Hispanic-origin groups presented in this chapter will not sum to totals because data for the "other races" group are not presented and Hispanics are included in both the white and black population groups. The NLSY97 data presented in chapter 3 are not strictly comparable, as they report mutually exlcusive categories of white (non-Hispanic), black (non-Hispanic), and Hispanic origin.

[6] Annual income figures are available only from the March supplement. Therefore, employment-population ratios shown in table 4.3 also are derived from the March supplement. As a result of the small 1-month sample size, the variances of these ratios are higher than those of annual averages or 3-year averages presented elsewhere in the article. Rates should be used to discern patterns by income group. Pooled data are a better source of information for overall representations of youths' work activity.

[7] For information on high school dropout rates and reasons, see *Dropout Rates in the United States: 1998* (Washington, National Center for Education Statistics, December 1, 1999). Also, see *A Comparison of High School Dropout Rates in 1982 and 1992* (Washington, National Center for Education Statistics, October 1996). Both reports are available on the NCES Internet site at **http://nces.ed.gov**.

[8] The text table shows comparisons for those groups with at least 50,000 youths (weighted count) in the labor force (employed plus unemployed).

[9] Data on country of birth have been available since the 1994 redesign of the CPS. Data discussed are pooled for 1994-98 to maximize the sample.

[10] For a discussion of the labor force characteristics of foreign-born workers, see Joseph R. Meisenheimer, "How do immigrants fare in the U.S. labor market?" *Monthly Labor Review*, December 1992, pp. 3-19.

[11] In 1996, Congress amended the Fair Labor Standards Act, creating Section 6(g)(1), which allows employers to pay any employee who is under age 20 a minimum wage of $4.25 per hour during the employee's first 90 calendar days of employment.

[12] The $5.57 median in 1998 can be compared with $4.96 in 1989 and $6.21 in 1979. The 1979 minimum wage of $2.90 is equal to $6.10 in 1998 dollars. The CPI-U-RS is used to adjust these figures. This research index is discussed in Kenneth Stewart and Stephen Reed, "CPI research series using current methods, 1978-98," *Monthly Labor Review*, June 1999, pp. 29-38.

[13] Historical changes to the minimum wage are presented on the Department of Labor, Employment Standards Administration website on the Internet at: **http://www.dol.gov/dol/esa/public/minwage/chart.htm**.

[14] Occupational data from the 1977-79 period are not reported due to major changes in the occupational classification system starting in the CPS in 1983.

Tab e 4.1. **Employment-population ratios of persons 15 to 17 years of age by selected characteristics, school and summer months, 1977-79, 1987-89, and 1996-98**

Sex age race and Hispanic origin	School months			Summer months		
	1977 79	1987 89	1996 98	1977 79	1987 89	1996 98
Total 15 to 17 years	29 8	27 6	24 7	42 6	39 6	33 8
Male	31 4	27 4	24 3	47 7	41 8	34 3
Female	28 1	27 9	25 2	37 4	37 4	33 3
Age 15	17 3	13 7	9 4	29 9	24 5	17 7
Age 16	29 5	27 7	25 8	43 2	41 4	36 0
Age 17	42 6	40 4	39 0	54 5	51 9	47 8
White 15 to 17 years	33 2	30 9	27 8	46 1	43 3	37 6
Male	34 8	30 5	27 3	51 2	45 3	38 1
Female	31 5	31 2	28 4	40 8	41 3	37 0
Black 15 to 17 years	10 7	12 9	12 8	22 8	23 8	20 1
Male	12 3	13 4	12 0	27 4	27 2	20 0
Female	9 2	12 4	13 7	18 2	20 3	20 2
Hispanic origin 15 to 17 years	19 8	17 1	14 6	30 4	24 2	19 6
Male	23 5	18 9	15 4	34 6	26 7	22 1
Female	15 7	15 3	13 7	26 4	21 8	16 7

NOTE School months are January to May and September to December Summer months are June July and August

Tab e 4.2. **Unemployment rates of persons 15 to 17 years of age by selected characteristics, school and summer months, 1977-79, 1987-89, and 1996-98**

Sex age race and Hispanic origin	School months			Summer months		
	1977 79	1987 89	1996 98	1977 79	1987 89	1996 98
Total 15 to 17 years	19 1	18 3	18 7	19 6	18 2	19 1
Male	19 6	19 8	20 2	18 6	18 3	20 2
Female	18 6	16 6	17 1	20 9	18 1	17 8
Age 15	17 4	19 1	23 5	19 6	19 0	21 9
Age 16	22 3	20 7	21 2	20 9	19 7	20 3
Age 17	17 5	16 2	15 6	18 6	16 7	17 0
White 15 to 17 years	17 1	16 2	16 5	16 7	15 5	16 2
Male	17 7	17 9	18 0	16 0	15 5	17 2
Female	16 4	14 4	14 8	17 7	15 4	15 1
Black 15 to 17 years	44 3	37 3	35 0	43 3	35 9	37 0
Male	42 6	36 9	37 1	40 1	35 0	39 4
Female	46 4	37 7	32 9	47 5	37 0	34 4
Hispanic origin 15 to 17 years	28 8	27 2	29 5	28 7	30 2	30 4
Male	26 1	27 3	29 6	29 2	30 5	28 9
Female	32 8	27 2	29 3	28 0	29 9	32 5

NOTE School months are January to May and September to December Summer months are June July and August

Table 4.3. **Employment status of persons 15 to 17 years of age by family income in previous year, March 1980, 1990, and 1999**

Indicator and characteristic	Total in families	Family income in 1998 dollars			
		Less than $27 300	$27 300 $50 999	$51 000 $79 999	More than $79 999
Employment-population ratio					
Total 15 to 17 years March 1999	23 9	15 0	22 1	29 5	29 5
Male	23 3	14 2	21 5	29 0	28 5
Female	24 6	15 9	22 6	30 0	30 5
Age 15	9 7	6 2	9 7	12 1	10 9
Age 16	24 8	16 0	21 8	32 3	29 7
Age 17	37 0	23 1	36 1	42 3	45 6
White 15 to 17 years	26 9	17 3	25 4	32 1	30 4
Black 15 to 17 years	11 9	9 9	8 5	16 9	21 4
Hispanic origin 15 to 17 years	14 6	10 9	15 4	19 6	22 1
Total 15 to 17 years					
March 1990	26 6	16 5	27 0	29 7	35 3
March 1980	28 4	17 6	26 8	34 5	36 9
Unemployment rate					
Total 15 to 17 years March 1999	18 7	30 6	22 8	13 9	12 0
Male	20 1	34 7	24 8	13 7	13 1
Female	17 1	26 3	20 7	14 2	10 9
Age 15	22 3	37 1	27 7	15 8	9 5
Age 16	20 8	29 9	31 0	11 1	15 1
Age 17	16 2	29 1	14 3	15 4	10 5
White 15 to 17 years	16 4	26 8	18 9	12 9	12 5
Black 15 to 17 years	38 5	45 0	51 9	26 3	11 1
Hispanic origin 15 to 17 years	24 1	32 4	20 8	19 9	11 8
Total 15 to 17 years					
March 1990	17 8	29 6	18 9	15 2	9 9
March 1980	19 3	30 1	20 5	16 3	13 1

NOTE   Income divisions were determined using quartiles in 1998   Divisions for earlier years were determined by deflating 1998 income categories by the CP U RS

Table 4.4. **Employment of persons 15 to 17 years of age by school enrollment status and selected characteristics, October 1977-79, 1987-89, and 1996-98**

Sex age race and Hispanic origin	Enrolled in high school			Recent dropouts		
	1977 79	1987 89	1996 98	1977 79	1987 89	1996 98
Total 15 to 17 years (in thousands)	10 882	9 398	10 902	295	200	281
Employment-population ratio						
Total 15 to 17 years (percent)	30 3	29 2	25 8	42 0	35 6	31 7
Male	32 0	28 6	25 4	54 4	47 9	40 1
Female	28 6	29 9	26 1	31 6	25 8	23 6
Age 15	18 1	15 8	10 5			
Age 16	31 8	30 6	27 4	28 6	30 5	30 3
Age 17	43 5	41 3	40 5	47 4	39 4	35 2
White 15 to 17 years	34 0	32 4	28 8	44 2	38 0	35 8
Male	35 6	31 9	28 3	56 0	51 6	45 0
Female	32 4	32 9	29 3	34 0	27 0	26 3
Black 15 to 17 years	9 6	14 6	14 4			
Hispanic origin 15 to 17 years	18 2	16 7	13 7		31 2	35 5

NOTE   Dash indicates data not shown where base is less than 50 000
Recent dropouts are persons who dropped out of high school between October of the survey year and the previous October

Tab e 4.5. **Average hours at work per week of persons 15 to 17 years of age by selected characteristics, school and summer months, 1977-79, 1987-89, and 1996-98**

Sex age race and Hispanic origin	School months			Summer months		
	1977 79	1987 89	1996 98	1977 79	1987 89	1996 98
Total 15 to 17 years	17 4	16 5	16 5	26 7	24 7	23 0
Male	18 7	17 4	17 2	28 4	25 8	24 2
Female	16 0	15 6	15 8	24 5	23 3	21 6
Age 15	11 7	11 6	11 6	21 9	20 3	18 9
Age 16	16 3	15 5	15 7	26 2	24 0	22 4
Age 17	20 6	18 6	18 2	29 7	27 1	24 9
White 15 to 17 years	17 4	16 4	16 4	26 9	24 7	23 0
Male	18 8	17 3	17 1	28 7	25 9	24 3
Female	15 9	15 4	15 6	24 5	23 2	21 5
Black 15 to 17 years	17 8	17 7	18 1	25 0	24 7	22 8
Male	17 8	18 1	18 2	24 6	24 9	23 7
Female	17 6	17 3	18 1	25 5	24 5	21 9
Hispanic origin						
15 to 17 years	21 8	21 4	21 0	28 5	27 3	25 1
Male	22 8	22 4	22 3	29 3	28 3	26 2
Female	20 2	20 2	19 3	27 4	26 1	23 4

NOTE School months are January to May and September to December Summer months are June July and August

Tab e 4.6. **Median hourly earnings of employed wage and salary workers 15 to 17 years of age paid hourly rates by selected characteristics, annual averages, 1998, 1989, and 1979**

Sex age race and Hispanic origin	Total paid by the hour in 1998 (in thousands)	Median hourly earnings (constant 1998 dollars)		
		1998	1989	1979
Total 15 to 17 years	2 908	$5 57	$4 96	$6 21
Male	1 430	5 60	5 09	6 33
Female	1 477	5 54	4 83	6 07
Age 15	353	5 38	4 69	5 60
Age 16	980	5 52	4 89	6 18
Age 17	1 574	5 65	5 08	6 34
White 15 to 17 years	2 558	5 57	4 96	6 20
Male	1 259	5 61	5 10	6 34
Female	1 298	5 54	4 80	6 05
Black 15 to 17 years	264	5 47	4 81	6 24
Male	123	5 43	4 77	6 20
Female	140	5 51	4 86	6 29
Hispanic origin 15 to 17 years	248	5 59	5 24	6 30
Male	140	5 73	5 29	6 34
Female	108	5 41	5 17	6 25

Table 4.7. **Employed persons 15 to 17 years of age by class of worker and selected characteristics, school and summer months, 1996-98, 1987-89, and 1977-79**

Sex age race and Hispanic origin	School months				Summer months			
	Total employed (in thousands)	Percent distribution			Total employed (in thousands)	Percent distribution		
		Wage and salary workers	Self employed workers	Unpaid family workers		Wage and salary workers	Self employed workers	Unpaid family workers
1996-98								
Total 15 to 17 years	2 896	97 1	2 3	0 6	3 969	95 9	3 3	0 8
Male	1 460	96 3	2 9	0 8	2 070	94 7	4 3	1 1
Female	1 437	97 8	1 8	0 3	1 899	97 2	2 2	0 6
Age 15	366	92 3	6 3	1 4	694	90 3	8 2	1 4
Age 16	1 011	97 2	2 2	0 6	1 412	96 0	3 0	0 9
Age 17	1 520	98 1	1 4	0 4	1 862	97 9	1 6	0 5
White 15 to 17 years	2 569	97 0	2 4	0 6	3 474	95 7	3 5	0 8
Black 15 to 17 years	240	98 8	1 3	0 0	376	98 4	1 3	0 5
Hispanic origin 15 to 17 years	225	97 3	1 8	0 9	309	96 8	1 6	1 6
Total 15 to 17 years								
1987 89	2 926	97 0	2 0	1 0	4 203	96 2	2 4	1 4
1977 79	3 696	95 0	2 8	2 2	5 274	94 5	2 4	3 1

NOTE School months are January to May and September to December Summer months are June July and August

Table 4.8. **Distribution of employed persons 15 to 17 years of age by industry and sex, school and summer months, 1977-79, 1987-89, and 1996-98**

ndustry	School months			Summer months		
	1977 79	1987 89	1996 98	1977 79	1987 89	1996 98
Total 15 to 17 years	100 0	100 0	100 0	100 0	100 0	100 0
Agriculture	6 4	4 5	4 8	10 6	7 7	7 7
Mining construction and manufacturing	10 9	6 5	5 6	12 7	8 4	6 7
Retail	48 2	58 9	61 6	37 4	47 7	51 1
Eating and drinking places	21 9	28 2	31 9	18 2	24 2	27 1
Other retail	26 3	30 7	29 7	19 2	23 5	24 0
Services	29 3	25 7	24 2	31 5	30 1	29 7
Other industries	5 1	4 2	3 8	7 8	6 1	4 7
Male 15 to 17 years	100 0	100 0	100 0	100 0	100 0	100 0
Agriculture	9 9	7 2	7 7	14 5	12 1	12 1
Mining construction and manufacturing	16 2	9 7	9 0	18 3	12 7	10 4
Retail	47 9	59 3	59 9	34 8	44 7	47 7
Eating and drinking places	19 4	27 5	31 3	14 5	21 4	25 7
Other retail	28 6	31 7	28 6	20 3	23 4	22 0
Services	20 5	19 4	19 4	24 0	24 0	24 4
Other industries	5 6	4 4	4 1	8 5	6 5	5 3
Female 15 to 17 years	100 0	100 0	100 0	100 0	100 0	100 0
Agriculture	2 4	1 8	1 9	5 4	2 6	3 0
Mining construction and manufacturing	5 1	3 3	2 2	5 4	3 4	2 7
Retail	48 6	58 6	63 4	40 7	51 2	54 9
Eating and drinking places	24 9	29 0	32 6	22 9	27 5	28 6
Other retail	23 7	29 6	30 8	17 8	23 7	26 3
Services	39 4	32 2	29 0	41 3	37 1	35 6
Other industries	4 6	4 1	3 4	7 2	5 7	3 8

Other industries include transportation communication and utilities and sanitary services; wholesale trade; finance insurance and real estate; and public administration

NOTE School months are January to May and September to December Summer months are June July and August ndustry detail may not sum to 100 due to rounding

Tab e 4.9. **Industries that employ the largest share of employed persons 15 to 17 years of age by sex, school months, 1996-98**

ndustry	Percent of total employed youths
Male	
Eating and drinking places	31 3
Grocery stores	13 6
Miscellaneous entertainment and recreation services	4 5
Agricultural production livestock	3 6
Construction	3 6
Department stores	3 1
Landscape and horticultural services	2 2
Newspaper publishing and printing	1 9
Agricultural production crops	1 5
Gasoline service stations	1 3
Female	
Eating and drinking places	32 6
Grocery stores	9 9
Private households	5 7
Department stores	4 4
Miscellaneous entertainment and recreation services	4 0
Stores apparel and accessory except shoe	3 6
Drug stores	1 9
Nursing and personal care facilities	1 7
Retail bakeries	1 5
Child day care services	1 4

NOTE   School months are January to May and September to December

Table 4.10. **Distribution of employed persons 15 to 17 years of age by occupation and sex, school and summer months, 1987-89 and 1996-98**

Occupation	School months		Summer months	
	1987 89	1996 98	1987 89	1996 98
Total 15 to 17 years	100 0	100 0	100 0	100 0
Executive professional and technical	2 4	3 3	2 5	2 9
Sales	24 3	27 3	18 7	21 9
Cashiers	12 0	16 9	9 7	13 6
Other sales	12 3	10 5	9 0	8 3
Administrative support including clerical	7 9	7 6	7 8	7 9
Service	40 2	38 8	39 5	39 9
Food preparation and service	25 3	27 4	22 1	24 0
Other service	14 8	11 4	17 4	15 9
Precision production operators and transportation	5 3	4 5	6 3	5 0
Handlers and laborers	13 9	12 9	13 7	12 4
Farm forestry and fishing	6 0	5 6	11 6	9 9
Male 15 to 17 years	100 0	100 0	100 0	100 0
Executive professional and technical	2 2	3 1	2 5	3 0
Sales	14 6	17 7	10 5	13 2
Cashiers	5 0	9 6	4 1	7 1
Other sales	9 6	8 2	6 4	6 1
Administrative support including clerical	4 4	4 3	4 1	4 4
Service	35 9	37 1	32 0	35 3
Food preparation and service	26 4	28 7	21 0	23 8
Other service	9 5	8 3	11 0	11 6
Precision production operators and transportation	8 5	7 3	9 5	7 9
Handlers and laborers	24 2	21 4	22 5	20 3
Farm forestry and fishing	10 2	9 1	18 9	15 8
Female 15 to 17 years	100 0	100 0	100 0	100 0
Executive professional and technical	2 6	3 3	2 5	2 8
Sales	34 2	37 1	28 3	31 4
Cashiers	19 1	24 3	16 2	20 7
Other sales	15 0	12 8	12 1	10 7
Administrative support including clerical	11 6	11 0	12 0	11 8
Service	44 6	40 5	48 2	44 8
Food preparation and service	24 3	26 1	23 4	24 3
Other service	20 3	14 5	24 8	20 6
Precision production operators and transportation	2 0	1 8	2 4	1 9
Handlers and laborers	3 4	4 4	3 4	3 9
Farm forestry and fishing	1 7	1 9	3 1	3 5

NOTE School months are January to May and September to December Summer months are June July and August

Occupational data from the 1977 79 period are not reported due to major changes in the occupational classification system starting in the CPS in 1983

Occupation detail may not sum to 100 due to rounding

Tab e 4.11. **Occupations that employ the largest share of employed persons 15 to 17 years of age by sex, school months, 1996-98**

Occupation	Percent of total employed youths
Male	
Stock handlers and baggers	13 4
Cooks	12 0
Cashiers	9 6
Waiters and waitresses assistants	5 2
Miscellaneous food preparation occupations	5 1
Farm workers	4 7
Janitors and cleaners	4 2
Food counter fountain and related occupations	3 5
Groundskeepers and gardeners except farm	3 3
Sales workers other commodities	2 3
Female	
Cashiers	24 3
Food counter fountain and related occupations	6 5
Waiters and waitresses	6 4
Sales workers other commodities	5 1
Child care workers private household	4 9
Cooks	4 4
Stock handlers and baggers	3 3
Sales workers apparel	3 2
Supervisors food preparation and service occupations	3 1
Waiters and waitresses assistants	2 9

NOTE School months are January to May and September to December

Appendix: A Comparison of CPS and NLSY97 Information about Youth Employment

Chapters 3 and 4 present information on youth employment from the National Longitudinal Survey of Youth 1997 (NLSY97) and the Current Population Survey (CPS), respectively. Table 4.A1 includes the percent of youths employed from table 3.1 in chapter 3 (NLSY97 data) and table 4.1 in chapter 4 (CPS data). According to the CPS, during the 1996-98 period, an average of 18 percent of 15-year-olds worked during summer months and 9 percent worked during school months. By comparison, the NLSY97 estimated that 64 percent of youths had participated in some type of work activity at some point during the year they were aged 15.

Previous research also has found differences in youth employment data from longitudinal surveys such as the older National Longitudinal Survey (NLS) cohorts and cross-sectional surveys such as the CPS.[1] This appendix explores possible reasons for the differences in these estimates, and also provides some empirical evidence on their possible effects.

Reasons for the differences in youth employment between the CPS and NLSY97

Why do the two surveys exhibit such large differences in the employment-population ratios of youths at these ages? As discussed below, the divergence in estimates partly reflects differences in the concepts—especially the reference periods for employment—being measured by the two surveys. Also, differences in survey design—such as the degree of probing in the interview protocol, the use of personal or proxy respondents, and difference in the mode of data collection—may be contributing factors.

Different reference periods. A primary reason for the divergence is that data from the two surveys refer to very different reference periods. The data for the NLSY97 in table 4.A1 refer to the 52-week periods during which youths were aged 14 (the year between their 14th and 15th birthdays) and aged 15 (the year between their 15th and 16th birthdays). The youths essentially are asked whether they held a job during any of the 52 weeks they were, for example, aged 15. In contrast, data for the CPS survey (table 4.A1) refer to a 1-week period, the week before the survey. The 1-week measures, for which data are obtained each month in the CPS, are averaged for all 15-year-old youths for the months June through August, to derive summer estimates, or for January through May and September through December to determine school-month estimates. It is very reasonable that the incidence of employment from a 1-week measure is much lower than that from a 52-week measure. As the remainder of this appendix indicates, however, not all of the divergence is the result of the difference in survey reference periods.

Different interview protocols. Another reason for the divergence of the estimates in the two surveys is the use of different interview protocols. The NLSY97 has a specific youth employment focus. The interview includes substantial and repeated probes to fill in a detailed employment history, and it uses a calendar visual aid as a prompting device for the respondent.

The NLSY97 interview protocol defines two types of jobs to respondents: employee jobs (in which the youth has an ongoing relationship with a particular employer, such as working in a supermarket or restaurant) and freelance jobs (doing one or a few tasks without a specific "boss," for example, babysitting or mowing lawns or working for oneself).

In the NLSY97, respondents are first asked to list all employee jobs held from the age of 14 to the date of the interview. The interviewer fills out a calendar and shows it to the respondent to confirm all start and stop dates of employee jobs, as well as gaps within employee jobs. Substantial probing is done by the interviewer to ensure a complete calendar listing. Then, respondents are asked to list all freelance jobs held from the age of 14

Table 4.A1. Percent of youths employed

Age	CPS, 1996-98		NLSY97, 1994-97		
	Summer months	School months	All jobs	Employee jobs	Freelance jobs
14	-	-	57.2	23.8	42.8
15	17.7	9.4	63.7	37.6	39.8
16	36.0	25.8	-	-	-
17	47.8	39.0	-	-	-

NOTE: Dashes indicate data not available or small sample sizes.

to the date of the interview. Again, a calendar is used to confirm all start and stop dates of freelance jobs. The freelance measure is somewhat less specific than the employee jobs measure, as information on gaps within freelance jobs is not collected, due to the sporadic nature of these jobs.[2]

In contrast, the CPS survey does not have a specific youth focus. It is designed to gather a wide range of data for multiple members within the same household. Therefore, the question sequences for each respondent are shorter and the CPS does not provide the same level of detail on work histories as does the NLSY97. The monthly CPS survey protocol for measuring each household member's employment status is based on a short set of questions. These questions determine whether the household member (aged 15 or older) did any work for pay "last week" (the week before the survey), was temporarily absent from a job, or worked for no pay in a family business. Given this very different interview protocol, CPS and NLSY97 employment measures would be expected to differ.

Self versus proxy response. Another important reason employment measures may differ between the CPS and the NLSY97 is the use of self responses versus proxy responses. In the CPS, more than 90 percent of the time, a person other than the youth is the primary respondent (person who answers the CPS survey questions) for the household.[3] The NLSY97 survey is always answered by youths themselves.

Should this difference across the two surveys be expected to lead to differences in employment-population ratios? The literature suggests that it may. A study by Richard Freeman and James L. Medoff examined differences between mothers' reports of the employment of their teenage sons, and self-reports by these sons and found that mothers underreported the employment of their sons.[4]

Parents (or other household members) may not always be aware of the employment activities of their children, particularly if the employment is sporadic, as is often true with babysitting and yard work, common "occupations" of youths. Proxy respondents also may not consider such freelance jobs to be "real work." For these reasons, allowing proxy respondents in the CPS survey may cause youth employment to be underestimated.

Personal visit versus telephone survey administration. A fourth reason why the NLSY97 and CPS employment figures may differ is the use of personal visits versus telephone surveys. The NLSY97 is a personal-visit survey with very infrequent telephone interviewing. In the CPS, the personal-visit protocol is used during the large majority of first month-in-sample interviews and, to a lesser extent, in the fifth month-in-sample. Telephone interviewing is typical in subsequent interviews.[5] These different methods of survey administration, while appropriate to the purposes of the two surveys, may contribute to differences in the measures of youth employment in the NLSY97 and CPS. However, it is difficult to isolate the impact of this factor from the impact of different reference periods, different interview protocols, and self versus proxy response.

Measures of the impact of differences in the CPS and NLSY97 on youth employment rates

The possible contributions of the above factors to observed differences in employment-population ratios between the NLSY97 and the CPS are examined next. By construction, the NLSY97 has some unique survey elements that permit this type of examination. Three exercises explore these elements of the NLSY97 interview and isolate, to the extent possible, the impact of the reasons discussed above for the divergence in the employment-population ratio estimates from the CPS and the NLSY97 surveys.

Exercise 1: A comparison of the CPS section of NLSY97 to CPS monthly

estimates. Before the rather intensive probing questions on employment were asked in the 1997 NLSY97 interview, respondents were asked the CPS questions on labor force status. The reference period in the NLSY97 "CPS section" pertains to labor force activity during the prior week, which is not necessarily the week including the 12th, as in the CPS. Although not exactly identical, it is possible to compare the magnitude of differences in estimates between the two surveys when the actual question wording and reference periods are nearly the same.

Percent of youths employed, February-May 1997

Age	CPS— total sample	CPS— first month in sample	NLSY97 (CPS)
15	9.2	10.4	26.6
16	23.8	25.6	38.9

The tabulation above shows the percent of youths employed during a 1-week reference period, averaged over the months of February through May of 1997, as a majority of NLSY97 respondents were interviewed during those months. The NLSY97 estimate of 26.6 percent of youths employed at age 15 (1-week reference period) is much lower than the estimate for age 15 reported in table 4.A1 (63.7 percent), which uses a 52-week reference period. Differences between the NLSY97 and CPS are thus reduced considerably when the questions and reference period are the same. The difference in magnitude of NLSY97 and CPS estimates shown in the above tabulation decreases substantially from age 15 to age 16. Even for age 16, however, the estimates are statistically different across the two surveys. The numbers in column 2 refer to first month-in-sample, during which the CPS administered a personal-visit survey rather than a telephone survey. The use of first month-in-sample only (personal interview) slightly increases the CPS estimates.

This type of exercise also was carried out by Norman Bowers with the older NLS cohorts and the CPS. He, too, found differences in the incidence of youth employment between the CPS and NLS. He found that differences are more pronounced for youths aged 16 and 17 than for older youths, and for young people whose major activity in the prior week is school attendance than for those whose major activity is something else (such as working or looking for work).[6] Bowers suggested this may be due to the more marginal nature of the labor market activity of young teenagers and those whose major activity is attending school.

Although the employment figures in the tabulation above are based on nearly the same survey questions and are for the same reference period, the issue of self-report versus proxy still exists because NLSY97 responses are self reports and CPS responses are mostly proxy reports.[7] It is possible that proxy respondents in the CPS underreport youth employment because they do not consider the work activities of youths to be "real work," or are unaware of the timing of the employment of the youths.[8] Exercise 2 sheds some light on this issue.

Exercise 2: Use of NLSY97 data to examine the impact of self versus proxy response. The issue of self versus proxy reporting also can be explored using the NLSY97 survey data. The NLSY97 survey administered a screening interview to determine sample eligibility for the survey. The screening interview was conducted with a household informant, generally a parent, and included fairly simple questions on the current employment status of household members. Although the questions do not replicate the CPS questions, the reference period is similar, and the interview results permit a comparison of estimates of each youth's current employment status from the household informant proxy to the estimates self reported by the youth during the CPS portion of the NLSY97 interview.

In the first interview of the NLSY97, a screener questionnaire was administered to a household member

Percent employed the week of the 12th

Age and survey		Jan.-May, 1996	June-Aug., 1996	Sept.-Dec., 1996	Jan.-Apr., 1997
Aged 15:	CPS	8.5	18.2	10.0	8.9
	NLSY97	17.1	23.5	16.3	14.8
Aged 16:	CPS	24.6	36.9	27.5	23.4
	NLSY97	(¹)	(¹)	35.2	32.9

¹ Numbers not nc uded due to sma samp e s zes (the o dest b rth year n the NLSY97 turned 16 n 1996; thus, on y nformat on from the ater months n 1996 and ear y 1997 s nc uded).

aged 18 or older. The questionnaire gathered information on the dates of birth of household members, which were used to determine whether there were any youths present in the household who were eligible for the NLSY97 survey. In households with eligible youths, the household member also was asked for additional information about household members including the employment status of all household members *aged 16 and older*. The respondent was first asked how many weeks the household member worked in self-employment or for someone else for pay in the 1996 calendar year. The respondent then was asked to provide that household member's usual hours of work per week, and was asked whether that household member was "currently employed."

The youth respondent was asked a "CPS section" — questions that are taken nearly verbatim from the monthly CPS — at the beginning of the NLSY97 youth questionnaire. The interviewer asked whether the youth did any work for pay in the previous week. In addition, the youth provided an employee job history later in the survey.

The tabulation below shows household member response (proxy response) about whether the youth is cur-

Percent of youths aged 16 and aged 17 employed in week before the interview, 1997

Household member response	Youth response: CPS section	Youth response: employee job history
33.5	43.1	32.7

rently employed and two corresponding youth self reports: a report of whether one worked for pay in the week prior to the interview from the "CPS section" and a report of whether one worked in an employee job in that same week. The sample is restricted to include only youths who received the NLSY97 youth questionnaire 1 week after the screener questionnaire was administered. Thus, the data show employment-population ratios for the same 1-week reference period from reports of the household member and of the youth on youth employment. This enables us to examine differences in self versus proxy reporting of youth employment.

According to household member responses, 33.5 percent of youths ages 16 and 17 are currently working. In the "CPS section" of the NLSY97, 43.1 percent of youths reported being employed. And, finally, in the employee job history, 32.7 percent of youths reported being employed (in employee jobs) during that same week. The household member report matches well with the youth report regarding employee jobs, but *understates* employment based on the response to the CPS questions given by the youth (which should cover all jobs, including more casual/informal employment relationships). Thus, it is possible that the household member is not including freelance jobs in the report about youth employment. The question the household member receives is not exactly the same as the CPS question (it asks whether the youth is "currently employed," while the CPS asks whether the youth did "any work for pay"), but the results are suggestive. In particular, this exercise suggests that having a proxy respondent in the CPS survey may cause employment among youths to be understated due to underreporting of work of youths in freelance jobs.

Exercise 3: Using the NLSY97 data on employee jobs to simulate the CPS reference period. A variant of the approach in exercise 1 can also be used to hold the reference periods constant between the two surveys. Because the NLSY97 includes a week-by-week employee-job history starting at age 14, it is possible to use these data to determine the labor force status of each youth during the week including the 12th of each month—the CPS reference week.[9]

The numbers in the tabulation at the top of the prior page depict the percent employed during the reference week averaged over different months for both the NLSY97 and the CPS. In all cases, the NLSY97 employee job history shows a greater incidence of employment than do estimates from the CPS. The differences in magnitude are, however, not quite as great as in the tabulation in exercise 1, particularly for 15-year-olds. Unlike in exercise 1, the NLSY97 estimates presented in this exercise do not include freelance jobs, which are included in the CPS estimates.[10] To the extent that the CPS does a better job picking up employee jobs than freelance jobs, the CPS employment-population ratios are closer to the NLSY97 ratios reported on the top of the prior page than they otherwise would be. The differences that do remain are again probably due to the fact that the CPS relies mostly on proxy response and to the different interview protocols across the two surveys.

Expected differences in employment-population ratios as the NLSY97 cohort ages

In exploring the differences between CPS and NLSY97 estimates of employment-population ratios of youths, one of the key aspects that has not been explored is the possibility that the im-

Table 4.A2. Employment-population ratios, by age and sex , 1979-1998, monthly Current Population Survey and the CPS section of the NLSY79 interview

Year and nterv ew months	Ages	Tota (percent)		Men (percent)		Women (percent)	
		CPS	NLSY79	CPS	NLSY79	CPS	NLSY79
1979 (Feb. – May)	16–17	36.2	45.1	38.1	49.2	36.0	41.1
1983 (Jan. – Apr.)	18–19	45.9	52.1	47.0	54.1	44.9	50.1
1985 (Jan. – Apr.)	20–24	67.3	71.8	72.1	75.3	62.8	68.3
1990 (Ju y – Oct.)	25–29	76.7	81.2	85.7	88.7	68.0	74.1
1994 (Ju y – Oct.)	30–34	79.5	80.4	89.2	89.0	70.0	71.7
1998 (Apr. – Ju y)	35–40	81.4	83.7	90.8	90.7	72.3	76.4

pact of different survey methodology factors such as reference period, proxy versus self response, extent of probing, and mode of collection all interact importantly with the fact that employment spells at young ages tend to be frequent and of short duration. If, as respondents age, a very high percentage of employment spells are of relatively long duration, such longer spells of employment are less apt to be forgotten by respondents. This would be the case whether the respondent is a proxy or self respondent, or whether the interview is administered by phone or in person. In addition, as youths age, they are less likely to do freelance work and more likely to have "employee" jobs. Thus, not only may the proxy respondent be more aware of the household member's work, but he or she may also be more likely to consider it "real work."

As a result, we would expect the employment-population ratios for the NLSY97 cohort and similarly defined ratios for the CPS survey to converge as the cohort ages. To examine this possibility, we compare statistics from the CPS and from the "CPS section" of the National Longitudinal Survey of Youth 1979 interviews to see if the divergence between the CPS and the NLSY79 measures of employment-population ratios closed as the cohort aged.[11] Table 4.A2 shows the results. In the table, the statistics are calculated for particular months, years, and age groups. These choices reflect both the ages of the NLSY79 respondents in each interview year, and the months in which relatively large numbers of interviews took place with NLSY79 respondents of those ages. The table

reports the comparison of the CPS average estimates with NLSY79 CPS module estimates for these same age group/periods.

As the table indicates, there is substantial convergence between the employment-population ratios from the two surveys, especially by the time the NLSY79 cohort reached their thirties—although for women, a small but persistent difference between the estimates from the two surveys remains even at those ages.

Conclusion

Chapters 3 and 4 report information on employment among youths from the CPS and the NLSY97. Both surveys show similar employment patterns by gender, race, and ethnicity, but the NLSY97 survey estimates are consistently higher. This appendix discusses some reasons why the NLSY97 and CPS estimates differ. A key reason is that the NLSY97 employment figures reported in chapter 3 are for a longer reference period than are the CPS figures in chapter 4. In addition, the NLSY97 uses an interview strategy that includes more probing about employment among youths. NLSY97 interviews are also conducted with the youth only (no proxy response) and are mostly conducted in person (and not by telephone). These features may lead to much higher employment estimates in the NLSY97 than in the CPS.

The NLSY97 includes a "CPS section" with nearly the same series of employment questions used in the monthly CPS. Data from these questions make it possible to examine how CPS and NLSY97 youth employment estimates compare when both the questions and the reference period are nearly the same. In addition, by looking at only first month-in-sample data in the CPS, the interview method (conducted in person and not by telephone) can be held constant when comparing the two surveys. This exercise reduces differences in the overall youth employment estimates from the two surveys considerably. However, differences still remain.

The NLSY97 includes an employee job history that allows the calculation of employment estimates based upon the same 1-week reference period as in the CPS. Youth employment estimates that focus on employee jobs only in the NLSY97 and the nonself-employed in the CPS also show reduced

differences in estimates between the two surveys. However, NLSY97 estimates of youth employment are still higher. The very different interview strategies between the two surveys and the possibility that proxy respondents in the CPS are not always aware of the timing of youth employment may explain some of this difference. Also, while the impact of self versus proxy responses cannot be directly compared across the two surveys, evidence from the NLSY97 suggests that proxy respondents in general understate youth employment because they are less likely to include freelance jobs in their reports.

Perhaps the most suggestive evidence comes from the NLSY79 survey, which clearly demonstrates that,

despite all of their differing features, a cross-sectional survey such as the CPS and a longitudinal survey such as the NLSY79 yield very similar estimates as a cohort ages. It appears that it is the nature of employment among youths—often involving freelance jobs, and employment spells that are short and frequent—that leads to differing estimates. Proxy respondents—perhaps more likely to forget about shorter spells or to not regard certain types of freelance jobs as work—appear to be more reliable reporters of employment among their adult peers, whose jobs are more likely of longer duration and considered "real work."

This appendix was contributed by Donna Rothstein, a research economist with the Bureau of Labor Statistics, and Diane Herz, an economist also with the Bureau. The authors thank Karen Kosanovich and Michael Horrigan for helpful comments, and Alexander Eidelman and Curtis Polen for excellent research assistance.

[1] See Norman Bowers, "Youth labor force activity: alternative surveys compared," *Monthly Labor Review*, March 1981, pp. 3-18; and Richard B. Freeman and James L. Medoff, "Why Does the Rate of Youth Labor Force Activity Differ Across Surveys?" in Richard B. Freeman and David A. Wise, eds., *The Youth Labor Market Problem: Its Nature, Causes, and Consequences* (Chicago, The University of Chicago Press, 1982), pp. 75-114.

[2] The NLSY97 definition of work at a freelance job while aged 14 (while aged 15) reported in chapter 3 depends on whether the period between any freelance job's start and stop date spans any of the weeks the respondent was aged 14 (15). If, for example, the freelance job began

before the respondent turned 15 and ended after the respondent turned 16, then the respondent would be counted as working in a freelance job while age 15. This may overstate the incidence of youths working at freelance jobs.

[3] It is possible that a youth present at the time of the interview answered questions about her or his own employment status, even if she or he was not the primary household respondent.

[4] Freeman and Medoff, "Why Does the Rate of Youth Labor Force Activity Differ?"

[5] While personal visits are the preferred method of interview in the fifth month-in-sample interview, a significant proportion of households (more than 30 percent in 1998) are interviewed by telephone.

[6] See Norman Bowers, "Youth labor force activity." Bowers finds that differences in NLS-CPS employment estimates tend to decline with age.

[7] Self-reported CPS youth employment information is not examined separately here. This is due to small sample sizes and the possibility that youths who self report at these young ages are

systematically different from youths who do not self report.

[8] This could explain why the difference in the CPS and the NLSY97 estimates decreases from age 15 to age 16, as freelance employment also appears to decrease as youths age.

[9] Freelance jobs are not used in this calculation because gaps within freelance jobs are not collected, and thus we cannot determine the exact timing of this type of employment.

[10] While freelance jobs are excluded from the NLSY97 measure in the tabulation at the top of page 49, they are not excluded from the CPS measure. The reason is that it is difficult to identify in the CPS survey jobs that would have been classified as freelance in the NLSY97. CPS employment-population ratios would thus be even lower if all "freelance jobs" were excluded.

[11] The NLSY79 is a nationally representative sample of 12,686 young men and women who were aged 14 to 22 when first interviewed in 1979. Respondents were interviewed annually through 1994, and are now surveyed biennially.

Chapter 5.
Youth Employment in Agriculture

Introduction

As discussed in chapter 1, laws governing youth employment in agriculture are different from the laws governing youth employment in other sectors of our economy. Indeed, the disparate treatment of youths under the law stems from a time when most agricultural jobs were on small family-operated farms. While a significant proportion of agricultural work is still done by unpaid family workers, paid employment has become increasingly prevalent.

This chapter focuses on paid employment of youths in crop agriculture. Youths working in agriculture often face unusual challenges—poor living and working conditions, loss of educational opportunities, separation from parental supervision, and exposure to pesticides and other occupational hazards. Because the farmworker population is particularly difficult to find and survey, this chapter utilizes a unique data source—an employer-based survey that finds the workers at their place of employment, and administers a detailed questionnaire at a later time and location convenient to the worker.

About the Data

The National Agricultural Workers' Survey

The National Agricultural Workers' Survey (NAWS) is a national survey of paid farmworkers in perishable crops. NAWS collects extensive data from farmworkers about basic demographics, legal status, education, family size and household composi-

tion, wages and working conditions in farm jobs, and participation in the U.S. labor force. Information for this report was obtained through 13,380 interviews of workers in the United States by NAWS during Federal fiscal years 1993 through 1998.

Initially, NAWS was commissioned by the Department of Labor (DOL) as part of its response to the Immigration Reform and Control Act of 1986. The NAWS continues to monitor seasonal agricultural wages and working conditions. Since its inception, several other Federal agencies have participated in the development of the NAWS by contributing questions, answers to which would assist them in better serving their farmworker constituency.

NAWS interviews workers performing crop agriculture. The U.S. Department of Agriculture defines crop work to include "field work" in the vast majority of nursery products, cash grains, and field crops, as well as in all fruits and vegetables. Crop agriculture also includes the production of silage and other animal fodder. The population sampled by NAWS consists of all farmworkers in crop agriculture, even if performing seasonal services within year-round employment. The definition of field work generally excludes secretaries and mechanics, but includes field packers, supervisors, and all other field workers.[1]

How NAWS samples child farmworkers

There are two ways in which NAWS can be used to look at children farmworkers. First, among the NAWS

interviewees is a subset of youths aged 14 to 17 who were sampled at their worksites along with the adults interviewed. These workers constitute a random sample of 14- to 17-year-old farmworkers. Between 1993 and 1998, NAWS interviewed 951 of these minor teenage farmworkers.

Second, NAWS asks farmworkers who are parents about their minor children. This provides a sample of dependents under the age of 18 who were living with their farmworker parents when the parents were interviewed for NAWS. The sample of farmworkers' children used in this report includes 6,422 U.S.-resident children listed by their parents on the NAWS family inventory between 1993 and 1998.[2] NAWS asks about each listed household member's gender, age, place of birth, and relationship to the interviewed farmworker, as well as a brief series of questions about schooling, work, and migration.

NAWS does not directly interview children younger than 14 years of age. Due to time constraints, NAWS can ask parents for only a limited amount of information about their children. Therefore, while we do know whether the children of farmworker parents are, themselves, farmworkers, we know very little about level or type of workforce participation of children under the age of 14.

Because there are two different methods by which data are obtained on children who work in America's fields, the two groups of minors (teenagers who are interviewed as part of the farmworker population, and dependents of farmworkers who also do farmwork) are discussed separately in this chapter. First, the demographics and working conditions of teenage respondents to NAWS are explored. Information on the characteristics of dependent children of farmworkers who themselves participate in farmwork is presented at the end of the chapter.[3]

Overview of Teenagers Employed in Agriculture

NAWS finds that, between FY1993 and FY1998, 7 percent of all farmworkers were between the ages of 14 and 17. If this percentage is multiplied by the estimated 1.8 million farmworkers per year who worked in U.S. fields, then there were approximately 126,000 children aged 14 to 17 working on America's farms each year. Overall, minors accounted for 4 percent of the total weeks worked in crop agriculture. The percent of work they performed is lower than their percentage of the labor force because children worked fewer weeks, on average, than did adults (14 versus 25).

Who are the youths who work in agriculture?

A demographic portrait of teen farmworkers can be drawn from the NAWS sample of 14- to 17-year-old respondents. (See chart 5.1.) Most teens who worked in agriculture were older—three-fourths of those between the ages of 14 and 17 who worked in the fields were aged 16 and 17. Like their adult counterparts, most (84 percent) teenage agricultural workers were young men.

Unlike the adult farmworker population, which was predominately (77 percent) foreign-born, most (52 percent) teen farmworkers were born in the United States.[4] Most of the foreign-born minors working in agriculture did not come to this country as young children, but were recent arrivals. Of these foreign-born minor farmworkers, 3 in 4 (75 percent) came to the United States between the ages of 14 and 17, and 58 percent came at ages 16 or 17.

Many of the teens doing farmwork are *de facto* emancipated minors. More than one-half (54 percent) of the minor farmworkers do not live with a parent. Very few live without a parent but with some other member of their family. Overall, nearly half (48 percent) of the minor farmworker teenagers live in households without any member of their family.

The farmworker population is very poor—56 percent live in households below the Federal poverty threshold. Examination of the family income of teenage farmworkers reveals a bifurcated population, with half (50 percent) living in households with annual incomes below $10,000 and more than one-third (35 percent) in households with incomes over $25,000 annually.

(See chart 5.2.) The probable explanation for the relatively high proportion of minors in households with family incomes over $25,000 annually is that these teens are not from households reliant on farmworker incomes but rather from more middle-class rural families in which the teens participate in seasonal (likely summer) employment in agriculture.

Given the high poverty rates among farmworkers, surprisingly few participate in Federal public assistance programs. Very few farmworkers (2 percent) live in households receiving Temporary Assistance for Needy Families (TANF) or Aid to Families with Dependent Children (AFDC), and only 13 percent receive Food Stamps. Farmworker teens are ap-

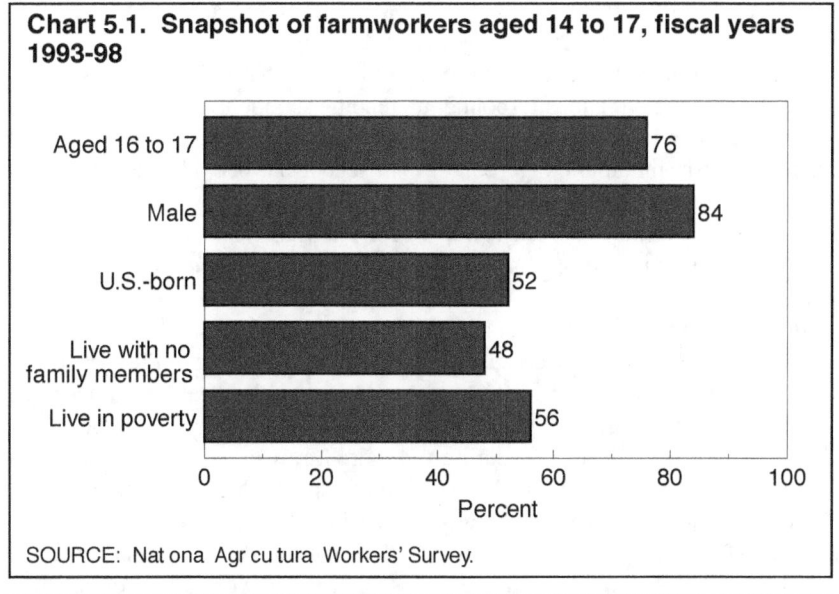

Chart 5.1. Snapshot of farmworkers aged 14 to 17, fiscal years 1993-98

SOURCE: National Agricultural Workers' Survey.

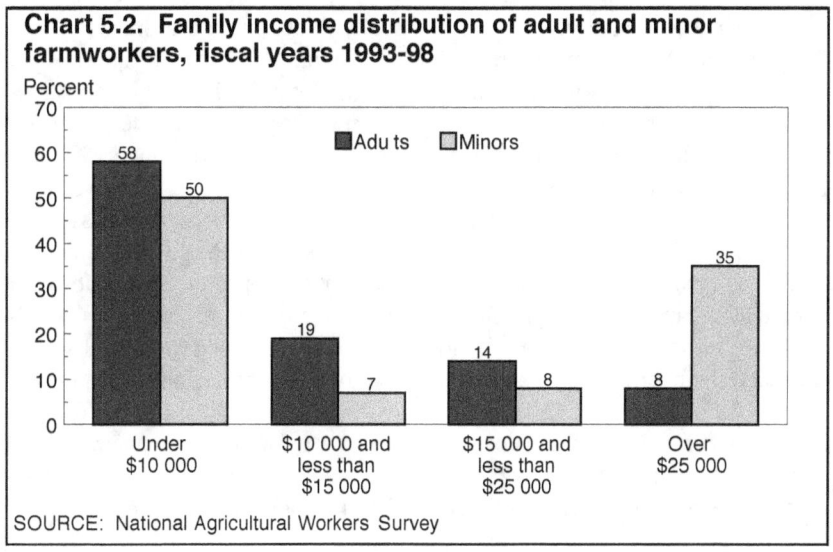

Chart 5.2. Family income distribution of adult and minor farmworkers, fiscal years 1993-98

SOURCE: National Agricultural Workers Survey

proximately half as likely to be in households receiving Food Stamps—only 7 percent of the farmworkers aged 14 to 17 are in households receiving this benefit.

Earnings and working conditions encountered by children who work

The people working in America's fields have some of the lowest-paying jobs in the country. Minors working in agriculture are paid even less than their adult counterparts. According to the NAWS data for 1993-98, teens were more prevalent in the lowest wage jobs. While 23 percent of adults earned minimum wage or less, 30 percent of teen farmworkers did so. Forty percent of adults and fifty percent of teens were paid between minimum wage and $1 over minimum wage. Adults were almost twice as likely to have the higher paying jobs. About 2 in 5 adults (37 percent) made more than $1 over the minimum wage, compared with only 1 in 5 minors.

In general, minors worked fewer weeks per year than did adults. Median weeks worked were 10 for minors and 24 for adults. Among minors, the average number of weeks worked was 14; however, there was considerable variation. One-third engaged in farmwork for 6 weeks or less during the year they were interviewed. However, 2 in 5 (40 percent) worked in agriculture for more than 13 weeks, indicating that they probably did some work during the school year.

Given their low pay and short time in the labor force, it is not surprising that teens have median annual earnings from agriculture that are substantially lower than those for adults. Nearly 3 in 5 teens (59 percent) earned less than $1,000 a year doing agricultural work, whereas half of the adults earned less than $5,000 in agriculture.

While teens earn less, there is no clear pattern in terms of working conditions. Similar proportions of adults and teens are paid by the piece (21 percent) and by the hour (77 percent). And, 21 percent of adults and 19 per-cent of minors work for farm labor contractors. Teens are less likely to pay for rides to work from a "raitero" (22 percent versus 38 percent). However, fewer teens report being covered by workers' compensation (63 percent versus 52 percent).[5]

Minor teen farmworkers differed from adults in the methods they used to find employment in agriculture. Teens were more likely than adults to find their jobs through friends, relatives, or workmates (82 percent versus 65 percent). Correspondingly fewer teens found their jobs on their own (11 percent versus 26 percent).

Well-being of child agricultural workers

The NAWS data show minor teens working in agriculture to be at high risk of never completing high school. Fewer than half (47 percent) were attending school at a grade level corresponding to their age, 15 percent were in school but behind in grade and 37 percent were drop-outs who did not have a high school diploma and had not attended school within the last year.

It is unlikely that many of these minor teenage farmworkers have employer-provided health insurance, because a very small proportion of the entire farmworker population (8 percent) reported having health insurance provided by their employers. More than one-fourth (26 percent) of minor teenage farmworkers reported difficulty in obtaining health care.

Migrant farmworkers have an even harder time surviving than do settled farmworkers.[6] NAWS defines a migrant as a person who travels 75 miles or more to do or seek farmwork. By this definition, teens were less likely to be migrants than were adults (36 percent versus 51 percent). However, those teens who are migrants live in very difficult conditions, usually without family supervision. According to NAWS, 4 in 5 migrant teens (80 percent) were *de facto* emancipated minors—not living with any other family member. The vast majority (91 percent) of minor migrant teens were foreign-born.

The Children of Farmworkers

Parents taking children to the fields

Very few children of farmworkers worked in the fields alongside their parents. During the period studied, only 6 percent of the U.S. resident children of farmworkers did farmwork. The other 94 percent of farmworker children did not go to the fields to work. NAWS did not ask parents detailed questions about the amount of work done by dependent children. If these children had worked amounts similar to the children sampled directly by NAWS, less than 1 percent of farmwork would have been done by children accompanying their parents to the fields.

Few children work in the fields with their parents because most children of farmworkers are very young—more than 4 out of 5 (83 percent) are under the age of 14 and 2 in 5 (40 percent) are under the age of 6. (See chart 5.3.) Farmworkers tend to have young children because most farmworkers themselves are fairly young. According to NAWS data, the median age of farmworkers was 28 years, and two-thirds of all farmworkers were less than 34 years old. This age composition of the farm labor force is likely to continue, as the workforce is continually replenished by young, new-immigrant workers.[7]

Younger children are less likely than teens to work alongside their parents. According to NAWS, approximately 3 in 10 (31 percent) 16- and 17-year-olds were working in the fields as were 2 in 10 (18 percent) 14- and 15-year-olds. Farmwork is much rarer among children under the age of 14. Only 3 percent of 6- to 13-year-olds and virtually none of the children under 6 were reported by their parents to have worked in the fields. However, the fact that parents report that their small children (aged 0 to 5 years) do not do farmwork does not mean that these children do not go to the fields. The parents of 7 percent of children aged 0 to 5 said that, sometime in the last 12 months, these children had accompanied them to the fields while they were working.

The next generation: farmworker children of farmworkers
Most (73 percent) of the children of farmworkers who themselves work in the fields are over the age of 13. Fourteen- and fifteen-year-olds make up 28 percent of farmworkers' children who do farmwork and sixteen- and seventeen-year-olds make up 45 percent. One factor that keeps more teens from going to the fields is that teenagers are often put in charge of their younger siblings. According to NAWS, 7 percent of teenagers (aged 13 to 17) were sometimes charged with the care of younger siblings while the parents were in the fields. Only 1 in 4 children working alongside parents in the fields is under the age of 14. In contrast, 86 percent of the children of farmworkers who do not work in the fields are under the age of 14, and 14 percent are 14 to 17 years old.

While three-quarters of the farmworker parents are foreign-born (73 percent), three-quarters of their children are U.S.-born (73 percent). Thus, most U.S.-resident children of foreign-born parents were born subsequent to

the parent's migration to the United States. Children who work in the fields along with their parents are more likely to be foreign-born than are those who do not (40 percent versus 24 percent).

Male children are more likely to work in the fields than are female children. While 52 percent of farmworker children are boys, they comprise 61 percent of the farmworker children of farmworkers.

Wages and family income
Children whose parents are paid a piece rate are more likely to work in the fields than are children whose parents are paid by the hour. While most children have parents who are paid by the hour (77 percent), 39 percent of children who work in the field have parents who are paid by the piece as compared to 18 percent of the children who do not work.

Almost two-thirds of farmworker families with U.S.-resident dependent children are poor (64 percent). While only 6 percent of U.S.-resident children of farmworkers are themselves farmworkers, families in which children work are more often poor than are other families (70 percent versus 64 percent).[8] This is an indication that children's earnings may be important to family incomes. Despite the difference in poverty rates, family incomes

are similar between families in which children work and those in which they do not. Families whose children work have more dependents at similar income levels, which results in higher poverty rates. Only 13 percent of U.S.-resident dependent children of farmworkers live in families with incomes of $25,000 or more; 27 percent live in families with incomes of $15,000 to $25,000 and 60 percent live in families with incomes under $15,000.

Despite the low levels of income and the high number of U.S.-born children, the use rate of needs-based assistance is much lower for the paid farmworker population than the corresponding poverty rate. While 70 percent of children who work lived in families with incomes below the Federal poverty guidelines, in the 2 years before the NAWS interview, only 46 percent of the children's families received Food Stamps, 16 percent received assistance from the Women, Infants, and Children program, and 11 percent participated in TANF (or its predecessor, AFDC). Families in which children do not work generally had even lower rates of participation in Federal needs-based assistance programs. While 64 percent of these families are in poverty, only 33 percent received Food Stamps, 32 percent received assistance from WIC, and 7 percent participated in TANF. (The higher WIC rates for children who do not do farmwork results from the higher share of children under age 6 in this group.)

Migration
Children with a migrant parent were more likely to work than were children whose parents are settled. Twenty-seven percent of all farmworkers' children live in a house with a migrant parent. However, 44 percent of children who work in the fields have a migrant parent, compared with just 27 percent of the children who do not work. (Again, because only 6 percent of the children are farmworkers, the average for all children tends toward the average of the 94 percent of children who do not work, despite sig-

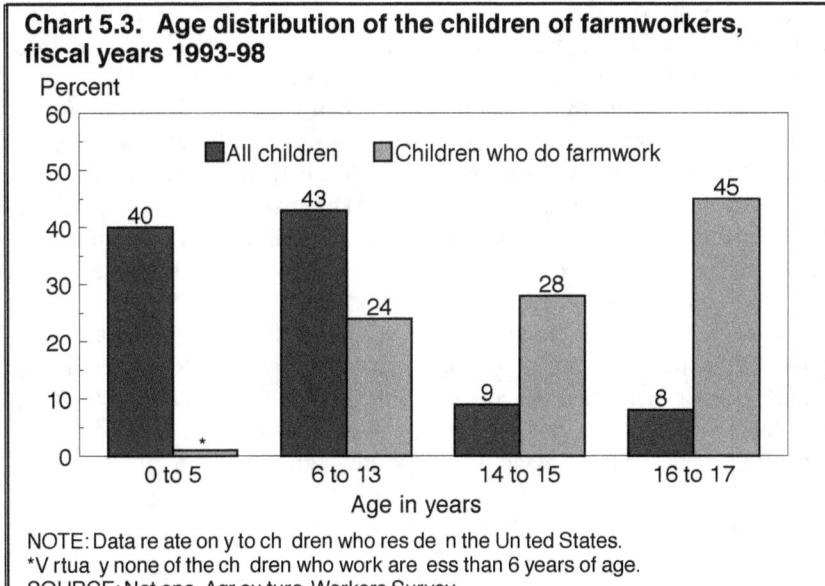

Chart 5.3. Age distribution of the children of farmworkers, fiscal years 1993-98

Percent

All children   Children who do farmwork

Age in years	All children	Children who do farmwork
0 to 5	40	*
6 to 13	43	24
14 to 15	9	28
16 to 17	8	45

NOTE: Data relate only to children who reside in the United States.
*Virtually none of the children who work are less than 6 years of age.
SOURCE: National Agricultural Workers Survey.

nificant differences between the two groups.) Children who work in the fields are more likely to migrate than are children who do not do farmwork. In almost all cases (99 percent), children who work in the fields accompany their migrant parent. However, children who do not work accompany their migrant parent only 55 percent of the time. The remainder of the time (45 percent), children who do not work are left behind when the parent migrates.

Health and education

While NAWS does not ask whether farmworkers have health insurance that covers their dependents, we know from interviewing the working parents that only 10 percent of the children of farmworkers had a parent covered by employer-provided health insurance. This rate was similar for children who worked in the fields and for those who did not. Unless parents participate in needs-based health insurance programs for their children to a greater extent than they participate in other needs-based programs, it is very likely that many of the children of farmworkers have no health insurance.

Most children of farmworkers had parents who said they found it easy to obtain medical assistance (71 percent).[9] However, more children who worked in the fields had parents who reported difficulty obtaining medical assistance (31 percent, versus 24 percent for children who did not work).

Almost one-fourth of school-age children of farmworkers are behind in grade or have dropped out of school. Of the children of farmworkers, those who worked in the fields were more likely to be behind in school. Only 62 percent of children who did farmwork were learning at grade level compared with 78 percent of those who did not do farmwork. Twenty-two percent of the children doing farmwork were behind in grade and 16 percent had dropped out.[10] While working in the fields may have affected their progress in school, children doing farmwork also had higher levels of other factors associated with being behind in school —they were more likely to be foreign-born and to be migrants.

Conclusion

An estimated 126,000 teens performed farmwork for wages each year from 1993 to 1998. While these teen farmworkers made up a small proportion of the farm labor force, and accounted for an even smaller amount of the total farmwork done, their situation merits serious attention. On average, teens who do farmwork earn less than $1,000 per year doing agricultural work; however, this income can be very important.

Three images of teen farmworkers come to mind. A small portion of teen farmworkers continue to be local rural youths whose parents are not farmworkers. These youths fit the traditional American image of students who work in the fields during school holidays. One example would be middle-class teens detassling corn in Midwestern farm communities.

However, while most teen farmworkers *were* born in the United States, the majority of them have characteristics that are very different from those of the aforementioned group. Overall, teen farmworkers are very poor—during the years covered by this chapter, more than half lived in households below the Federal poverty threshold. Most were from poor, often migrant households, with incomes under $25,000. Despite the high poverty levels in these households, very few were recipients of needs-based public assistance.

These less-advantaged teen farmworkers consisted of two groups. One group fit the traditional image—teens working along with their parents in the fields. In addition, this chapter identifies a new and growing group of teens who are "de facto" emancipated minors. These teens live and work on their own away from their families. These farmworker teens are falling behind academically. Nearly two-fifths worked in agriculture for more than 13 weeks in a year, indicating that they probably did some farmwork during the school year. Fewer than half of all teen farmworkers attended school at grade level and fully two-fifths were dropouts.

Whether or not they themselves do farmwork, many children living in farm-worker families were in difficult circumstances. The low wages and migratory nature of farmwork take their toll even on the farmworker children who do not work in the fields.

Most farmworkers are very young and, thus, their children also tend to be very young. Therefore, few children of farmworkers work in the fields alongside their parents. Six percent of the U.S.-resident children of farmworkers were themselves farmworkers. Of those, one-fourth were under the age of 14.

However, because farmworker families tend to be poor, having young children accompany their parents to the field may, in some cases, be the only childcare option. Unfortunately, having young children in the fields potentially exposes them to pesticides and other dangers inherent in farmwork. Parents of 7 percent of children aged 0 to 5 reported that their children had sometimes accompanied them to work in the fields.

Nearly two-thirds of farmworker families with U.S.-resident dependent children were poor. Among farmworker households in which children also were farmworkers, 70 percent were below the poverty threshold. Farmworker children of farmworkers were having difficulties getting an education. Twenty-two percent of the children doing farmwork were behind in grade, and 16 percent dropped out before graduating from high school.

This chapter was contributed by Ruth Samardick, a survey statistician with the Labor Department's Assistant Secretary for Policy. Susan M. Gabbard and Melissa A. Lewis, both of Aguirre International, helped to prepare the report.

[1] There are an estimated 1.8 million crop workers in the United States. This number is derived by adjusting the 1992 Commission on Agricultural Workers estimate of the total number of farmworkers (2 5 million, which includes livestock workers), by the proportion of hours worked in agriculture that can be attributed to crop agriculture (72 percent, a proportion extrapolated from two surveys conducted in 1997 by the U.S. Department of Agriculture—the Census of Agriculture and the Quarterly Agricultural Labor Survey).

[2] This number is weighted not only by NAWS post-sampling weights but also by an additional weight that accounts for the number of parents working in farmwork and thus the probability that a child was listed in the NAWS household inventory.

[3] Differences between groups reported in this chapter are significant at the 95-percent confidence level. In order to ensure statistical reliability, cells containing less than 50 observations are not reported.

[4] Between fiscal years 1990 and 1991, 80 percent of U.S.-born Hispanic farmworkers had a farmworker parent. However, most U.S.-born children of Hispanic farmworkers do not become farmworkers. See "Migrant Farmworkers: Pursuing Security in an Unstable Labor Market," Research Report No. 5 (Washington, U.S. Department of Labor, Office of the Assistant Secretary for Policy, May 1994).

[5] The proportion of workers claiming that they are covered by workers' compensation is likely less than the proportion of workers actually covered by law. However, worker responses about whether they are covered by workers' compensation is a good indicator of how many workers would know to insist on coverage in case of a work-related injury.

[6] See "Migrant Farmworkers."

[7] See Mines, Gabbard, and Steirman, "A Profile of U.S. Farmworkers: Demographics, Household Composition, Income and Use of Services," Research Report No. 6 (Washington, U.S. Department of Labor, Office of the Assistant Secretary for Policy, April 1997), pp. 3-5.

[8] Because of the large difference in the number of children who did farmwork compared with those who did not, averages for the entire population are most often determined by the average of the larger group. Nevertheless, individual characteristics, such as poverty rates, frequently differ significantly between the two groups.

[9] Five percent of the children's parents responded that they either did not know or did not remember whether it was easy or difficult for them to get medical assistance.

[10] Children were considered to be behind in grade if their grade minus their age was 7 or more. Dropouts were children 17 and under who had not been to school in the last 12 months and who had not completed 12 years of education.

Chapter 6.
Occupational Injuries, Illnesses, and Fatalities

Introduction and Overview

This chapter provides a statistical profile of risks to the safety and health of working youths. This information is important because the intent of much of the regulation of youth employment is to limit the exposure of working children to the risks of injury and death. Federal and State laws prohibit employment of youths in high-risk activities, such as driving, or operating other types of machinery. (More information on the Federal and State regulation of job risks encountered by youths is provided in chapter 2.)

A number of studies have addressed the problems of safety and health of young people on the job.[1] This chapter supplements this knowledge by presenting selected data on serious work injuries incurred by youths. The Bureau of Labor Statistics regularly collects data on serious work injuries of youths, but published data are usually restricted to the age group 16 to 19. This chapter includes previously unpublished BLS data on work injuries that either result in the death of a a youth, or require him or her to stay away from work to recuperate from the injury. Employment also can have serious long-term effects on health that are not immediately evident. For example, workers, whether young or old, may be exposed to high noise levels on the job that result in hearing loss later in life.[2] Our statistical profile does not include information on job risks with long latency periods.

The second section reviews sources of information about workplace injuries of youths generally, as well as

more detailed information about the Bureau's statistics used to construct the profile. Data on fatalities to youths in the workplace are collected in the BLS Census of Fatal Occupational Injuries (CFOI), an annual census covering all sectors of the U.S. economy. Annual data on injuries to youths resulting in lost workdays are collected in the BLS Survey of Occupational Injuries and Illnesses (SOII) for wage and salary workers in private industry. After reviewing what these data show about the characteristics of youth fatalities and lost workday injuries in the next two sections, the final section assesses the risks of injuries and illnesses to working youths compared to workers aged 25 to 44.

Profile summary for occupational fatalities

The BLS Census of Fatal Occupational Injuries shows that occupational fatalities to youths 17 and under varied between 62 and 70 per year from 1992 to 1998. For this period, 89 percent of these deaths occurred to young males; 29 percent of youths killed on the job were under the age of 15. Thirty percent of occupational fatalities among youths occurred while they were working in a family business, and a very high percentage of these fatalities—43 percent—occurred in agriculture.

To assess the risks of an occupational fatality to youths, the occupational fatality data for 15- to 17-year-olds and for workers aged 25 to 44, were compared with estimates of hours worked from the Current Population Survey (CPS) for these labor force groups. (Unfortunately, there are few

sources of information on hours worked to assess the risks to workers under 15 years of age.) These data indicate that the entire labor force of 15- to 17-year-olds, on average, incurred a risk of an occupational fatality per hour of work that was about 80 percent of the corresponding risk for the older workers. Agricultural employment is particularly dangerous work; youths aged 15 to 17 who have jobs in agriculture had a risk of a fatality that was more than 4.4 times as great as the average worker aged 15 to 17. The data also indicate that youths in agriculture face about the same risks of an occupational fatality as do adults aged 25 to 44 working in agriculture. The high concentration of youth fatalities in agriculture is also partly accounted for by the relatively longer hours they work in agriculture than elsewhere in the economy.

The estimates of risk of an occupational fatality to two relatively small groups of young workers also bear noting. First, youths in construction jobs had a risk of an occupational fatality per hour worked that was about twice the corresponding risk to all workers aged 25 to 44 in the construction industry during the period 1994 to 1998. Second, youths who were self-employed or working in a family business had a risk of an occupational fatality that was at least 4 times as great as that of other youths, regardless of industry.

Profile summary of lost work-time injuries

Data from the Survey of Occupational Injuries and Illnesses on the characteristics of injuries among youths that result in days away from work cover only wage and salary jobs in private industry and in large agricultural establishments. Almost all (97.3 percent) of these injuries to youths occurred to 16- or 17-year-olds. A summary measure of the severity of these injuries, median lost workdays, was about 4 days throughout the period 1992-97. Injuries to young workers resulting in lost workdays declined rapidly from 1995 to 1997; in 1997, such worktime injuries among youths comprised less than 1 percent of these injuries for the labor force as a whole. Commonly, these injuries include sprains, strains, and tears (more prevalent among young women) and cuts and lacerations (more prevalent among young men). Over the period 1992-97, the severity of lost workday injuries to young women became more similar to the severity of injuries to young men.

The distribution of lost workday injuries among youths generally follows the distribution of employment; more than 80 percent of these injuries occurred in either the retail trade or services industries in the 1992-97 period. Looking at variation in the risk of a lost worktime injury per hour worked among these industries, such risks were about 3 times as high in health services as in all retail trade and services jobs, on average.

BLS Sources of Information on Workplace Injuries of Youths

Comprehensive national data programs providing information on occupational injuries for youths separately were not developed until 1992. Since then, national data for youths have been available annually from two BLS programs: the Census of Fatal Occupational Injuries and the Survey of Occupational Injuries and Illnesses. Since 1972, the SOII has reported annually on the number of workplace injuries and illnesses in private industry and the frequency of those incidents. With the 1992 survey, BLS be-

gan collecting additional information on the more seriously injured or ill workers in the form of worker and case characteristics, including age. At that time, BLS also initiated a separate Census of Fatal Occupational Injuries to count fatalities more effectively than had been possible in the SOII.

CFOI is a Federal-State cooperative program, implemented in all 50 States and the District of Columbia. To compile counts that are as complete as possible, the census uses multiple sources to identify, verify, and profile fatal worker injuries. Information about each workplace fatality—occupation and other worker characteristics, equipment involved, and circumstances of the event—is obtained by cross referencing the source records, such as death certificates, workers' compensation reports, and Federal and State agency administrative reports. To ensure that fatalities are work-related, cases are substantiated with two or more independent source documents, or a source document and a follow-up questionnaire.

Establishments surveyed by SOII are asked to provide additional information for a sample of injuries in the workplace in the past year that involved at least 1 day away from work, beyond the day of injury or onset of illness. Employers provide several types of information about these cases, including the demographics of the worker disabled, the nature of the disabling condition, and the event and source producing that condition. There are several limitations of this survey

that are important for the measurement of work injuries to youths. Excluded from survey coverage are Federal, State and local governments, the self-employed and workers in their own family businesses, and agricultural enterprises with fewer than 11 employees. As shown in previous chapters, agriculture and family businesses are an important source of jobs for youths. The threshold for inclusion of cases in these data, not being able to return to work on the "next regular workday," may be higher for young workers as they are much more likely to work part time than is the rest of the labor force.

Characteristics of Work-related Youth Fatalities, 1992 to 1998

CFOI data indicate that an average of 67 work-related deaths per year occurred among youths under 18 over the period 1992 to 1998. (In contrast, the average annual number of occupational fatalities to all other workers—those 18 years or older—between 1992 and 1998 was 6,208.) Chart 6.1 shows only slight variation in youth fatalities, which hovered around the upper 60s during most of the period, except for 1997, when they dropped to the lower 60s. However, the total number of hours worked by youths has increased substantially over this period, so that the risk of a fatality occurring—per hour worked—has declined. In particular, analysis of unpublished CPS data indicates that total hours worked among 15- to 17-year-olds in-

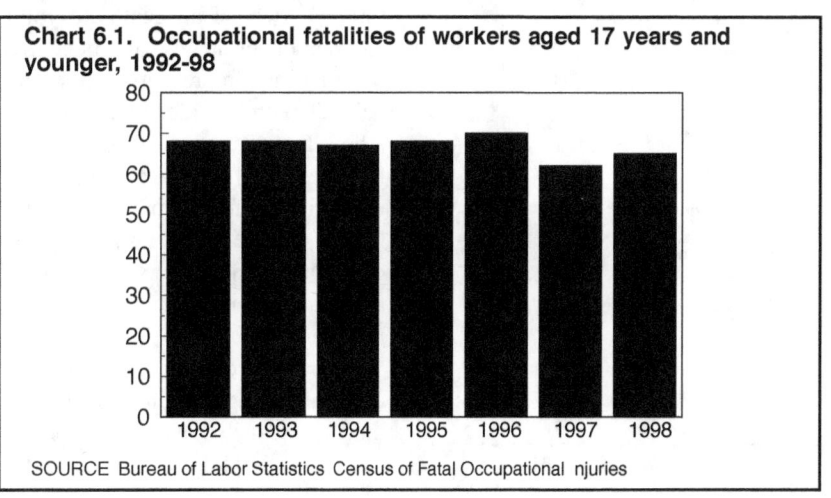

Chart 6.1. Occupational fatalities of workers aged 17 years and younger, 1992-98

SOURCE Bureau of Labor Statistics Census of Fatal Occupational njuries

creased by about 38 percent from 1992 to 1998. (Occupational fatalities also occur to youths under 15 years of age, but we have no information on hours worked to gauge the risk of a fatality for them.) Because the absolute numbers of occupational fatalities among youths are small, this chapter analyzes the characteristics of the total number of fatalities over 1992–98.

Table 6.1 presents data on selected characteristics of youths who died on the job over the 1992–98 period. These workers were predominantly males, about 89 percent of the total. Eighty-five percent of these workers were identified as white, and Hispanics represented 14 percent of the total youth fatalities. About 30 percent of the youth fatalities occurred while the deceased was working in family businesses. It is not possible to assess whether these fatalities are disproportionate to their representation in the labor force, as many of these workers are under 15 years of age. The CPS does not provide labor force participation data for youths younger than 15 and the National Longitudinal Survey of Youth does not cover the period of interest here. As shown in table 6.1, about 29 percent of occupational fatalities among youths under the age of 18 occurred among these very young workers.

Industry concentrations of occupational fatalities

Table 6.2 shows that the distribution of occupational fatalities among youths by industry contrasts sharply with the industry distribution of fatalities for all other workers. About three-fourths of the deaths of youths were concentrated in three industries: Agriculture, construction, and retail trade. As discussed below, these concentrations are only partly explained by industry concentrations of youth employment and hours worked; agriculture and construction youth employment, in particular, is associated with a high risk of a fatality. BLS has profiled youth fatalities in each of these three industries for the period 1992 to 1997.[3]

The characteristics of youth job fatalities in agriculture are quite distinctive in a number of ways. In agriculture they are more likely to occur among the youngest workers. About three-quarters of all deaths to young workers under the age of 15 occurred in agriculture, representing more than half of youth fatalities in agriculture.[4] About three-quarters of occupational fatalities in self-employed jobs were in the agricultural industries. More than half of the deaths in agriculture occurred in family businesses. Family farms are exempt from OSHA safety requirements.[5]

The most common cause of death of youths in agriculture is from farm machinery, such as a harvester or tractor. For example, the cases of work-related youth fatalities in Minnesota between 1994 and 1997 chronicled in the attached box illustrate the kinds of dangers youths can encounter in working with farm machinery. Nationwide, over the 1992–97 period, 51 deaths of youths in agriculture could be specifically attributed to involvement with tractors; in about half of these cases a tractor overturned on the youths.[6]

As shown in previous chapters, jobs in the retail trade industries, such as restaurants, grocery stores, or shops and department stores comprise one of the largest parts of youth employment. Of the total fatalities among youth in retail trade between 1992 and 1998, about two-thirds were homicides. Analysis of the circumstances of these homicides suggests that robberies were probably the cause of from one-fourth to one-half of all youth fatalities in retail trade.[7] Incidents involving transportation while working, such as highway crashes, were the next most frequent cause, accounting for 18 percent of youth fatalities in retail trade.

Table 6.2 shows that, nationwide, more work-related fatalities are reported in the construction industry than in other industries. Analysis of the fatalities of youths in construction indicates that the majority of these deaths occurred among those employed as construction laborers, particularly for special trade contractors (for example, roofing or concrete work) during the summer months.[8] The three most common events or exposures associated with these youth fatalities, comprising about 60 percent of the 64 deaths, were falls (such as

Table 6.2. **Occupational fatalities among youths under age 18 by major industry division, 1992–98**

Total	Youths under 18		All 18 and older	
	Counts	Percent	Counts	Percent
Agricultural forestry and fishing	200	42 7	5 595	12 9
Construction	64	13 7	7 195	16 6
Manufacturing	24	5 1	5 169	11 9
Transportation and public utilities	12	2 6	6 514	15 0
Wholesale trade	14	3 0	1 757	4 0
Retail trade	90	19 2	4 854	11 2
Services	38	8 1	5 355	12 3

SOURCE BLS Census of Fatal Occupational Injuries

Table 6.1. **Fatal occupational injuries to youths under age 18 by selected worker characteristics, 1992–98**

Characteristics	Counts	Percent
Sex		
Males	416	88 9
Females	52	11 1
Race/ethnicity		
White	399	85 3
Black	26	5 6
Asian or Pacific Islander	11	2 4
Other	32	6 8
Hispanic origin	67	14 3
Employee status		
Wage and salary workers	311	66 5
Self employed or family business	157	33 5
Working in family business	141	30 1
Age		
Under 15	134	28 6
15	54	11 5
16	100	21 4
17	180	38 5
15 to 17	334	71 4

NOTE Percentages may not add to totals because some categories are omitted

from roofs or skylights), electrocutions, and being struck by objects—particularly falling objects.[9]

Similarities in types of work-related fatalities between youths and older workers

Given the distinctive industry concentration of young workers, it might be expected that the types of events (for example, highway collision) or exposure (for example, electrocution) that are primarily associated with youth occupational fatalities would differ from breakdowns for older workers. However, across all industries the distribution of fatalities by event of exposure for young workers is fairly similar to those of all other workers.[10] Because occupational fatalities among youths are concentrated in agriculture, retail trade, and construction, comparisons

within these industries are also useful to examine. These comparisons are shown in table 6.3.

Transportation incidents (including collisions, overturned vehicles, or being struck by a vehicle) are a somewhat more frequent cause of fatalities for young workers in agriculture and construction than for other workers, but this is not the case for retail trade. Among these three industries, categorization of fatalities by event or exposure is most dissimilar between youths and other workers in construction. In retail trade, the preponderant cause of death is "assaults and violent acts." Somewhat surprisingly, the proportion of occupational fatalities among retail workers that are homicides is virtually identical among both younger and older workers—about two-thirds of all fatalities in each group.

Characteristics of Injuries and Illnesses with Lost Work Days, 1992–97

In 1997, the Survey of Occupational Injuries and Illnesses estimated that there were 11,248 cases of injuries resulting in lost workdays to private industry wage and salary workers aged 17 and younger, about 0.6 percent of the total of all such cases (1,833,380) in 1997. (See table 6.4.) Almost all these injuries to youths in 1997—97.3 percent—occurred among 16- and 17-year-olds. A summary measure for the severity of these injuries, the median days of work missed as a result of the injury, indicates that, overall, young workers have had less severe injuries than other workers have. Median workdays lost were 4 days for young workers, but 5 days for all other work-

Tab e 6.3. Distribution of fatal occupational injuries by event or exposure in agriculture, retail trade, and construction, 1992-98

Event or exposure by industry	Youths under 18		18 and older	
	Number	Percent	Number	Percent
Agriculture				
Total all events	200	100 0	5 594	100 0
Transportation incidents	114	57 0	2 847	50 9
Assaults and violent acts[2]	12	6 0	369	6 6
Contact with objects or equipment[3]	45	22 5	1 289	23 0
Falls[4]	6	3 0	418	7 5
Exposure harmful substances or environment[5]	18	9 0	576	10 3
Retail trade				
Total all events	90	100 0	4 854	100 0
Transportation incidents	16	17 8	985	20 3
Assaults and violent acts[2]	61	67 8	3 267	67 3
Contact with objects or equipment[3]	5	5 6	192	4 0
Falls[4]	3	3 3	174	3 6
Exposure harmful substances or environment[5]	4	4 4	145	3 0
Construction				
Total all events	64	100 0	7 195	100 0
Transportation incidents	20	31 3	1 826	25 4
Assaults and violent acts[2]			222	3 1
Contact with objects or equipment[3]	16	25 0	1 351	18 8
Falls[4]	16	25 0	2 288	31 8
Exposure harmful substances or environment[5]	12	18 8	1 286	17 9

ncludes highway collisions overturned vehicle fall from vehicle or struck vehicle
[2] ncludes homicides and assaults by animals
[3] ncludes being struck by object caught in or compressed by equipment or collapsing materials
[4] ncludes falling down stairs from loading docks roofs or scaffolding
[5] ncludes contact with electric current (electrocution) drowning exposures to toxic substances
NOTE Dash indicates data not available
SOURCE BLS Census of Fatal Occupational njuries

Tab e 6.4. Nonfatal occupational injuries and illnesses with days away from work by age, 1992-97

Year	Total all ages	All 17 and younger	Ages 16 and 17
1992	2 331 098	22 121	20 783
1993	2 252 591	21 620	20 708
1994	2 236 639	23 131	21 884
1995	2 040 929	19 507	18 625
1996	1 880 525	15 156	13 647
1997	1 833 380	11 248	10 946
Cumulative percent change 1992 97	21 35	49 15	47 33

SOURCE BLS Survey of Occupational njuries and llnesses

Tab e 6.5. Lost worktime injuries by industry, youths aged 17 and under, 1992 and 1997

ndustry	1992		1997	
	Number	Percent	Number	Percent
Total	20 783	100 0	10 946	100 0
Retail trade	14 161	68 1	7 658	70 0
Services	3 682	17 7	1 906	17 4
Manufacturing	1 046	5 0	454	4 1
Wholesale trade	488	2 3	288	2 6
Construction	323	1 6	233	2 1
Rest of private sector	1 083	5 2	407	3 7

ncludes mining transportation and public utilities finance insurance and real estate and agriculture establishments with more than 11 employees

SOURCE BLS Survey of Occupational njuries and llnesses

ers. The industry distribution of these injuries among young workers roughly follows the concentration of their wage and salary employment; more than 80 percent of these injuries occurred in either retail trade or services employment.[11]

1992–97 trends

Chart 6.2 shows how lost workday injuries among youths have changed from 1992 to 1997. The cumulative percent decline from 1992 to 1997 was 49 percent, but these injuries did not start to decline until 1995 and then decreased rapidly to 1997. In part, these declines reflect a trend toward an increase in workplace safety, as lost workday cases of those 18 and older also experienced a decline over the 1992-97 period. (See table 6.4.) Nevertheless, lost workday cases among youths have decreased more rapidly than the older group's and were a significantly smaller share of all lost workday cases in 1997 than 6 years earlier, despite the fact that, over this period, employment grew more among youths than among older workers.[12]

The reduction in lost worktime injuries among youths between 1992 and 1997 occurred in all major industries. Over this 6-year period, these injuries fell by almost half with little change in industry concentration. As table 6.5 shows, 70 percent of injuries occurred in retail trade establishments in 1997 and an additional 17 percent occurred in service industries that year. The industry concentration was similar in 1992. In the services industries, more than half the injuries occurred in health services and amusement and recreation (for example, amusement parks).[13]

Comparisons of severity of injuries

In the sampling of characteristics of injuries, SOII obtains the number of days away from work, thus providing an indicator of the severity of the injury. Table 6.6 compares the distribution of these days away from work be-

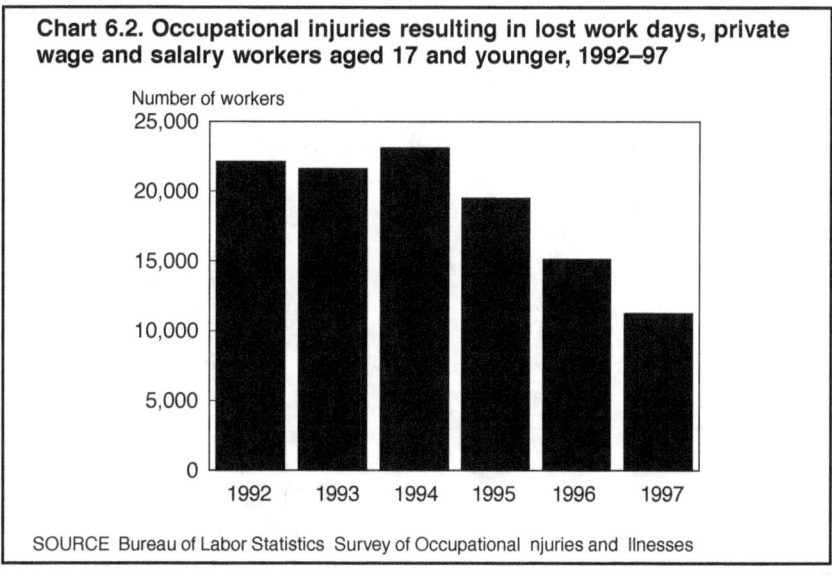

Chart 6.2. Occupational injuries resulting in lost work days, private wage and salary workers aged 17 and younger, 1992–97

SOURCE Bureau of Labor Statistics Survey of Occupational njuries and llnesses

tween youths and adults, and between male and female youths. These data indicate that injured adult workers have tended to lose more workdays than injured youths, and that the severity of all lost worktime injuries—but not those of youths—fell between 1992 and 1997.[14] In 1997, about 25 percent of all workers with lost workdays were away from work for more than 20 days (4 weeks or more on a full-time schedule), whereas about 10 percent of employed youths experienced this number of lost workdays. However, these data may overstate the relative severity of adult work injuries because youths are more likely to have short duration jobs or work intermittent schedules than adults. Twenty or more lost workdays represent a longer period of recuperation for workers on intermittent schedules, and injured workers with short duration jobs may have not had the opportunity to work many additional days.

Comparisons of the severity of injuries between young male and female workers may be less problematic. Their variation in the numbers of days away from work became more similar by 1997. In 1992, lost workday cases among young women were likely to result in just 3 median days away from work, compared with 4 days for young men. In 1997, both male and female youths experienced about 4 median days of lost worktime.

Common types of injuries among youths

The most frequent single type of injury resulting in lost worktime among youths under 18 is a muscle sprain, strain, or tear, usually resulting from overexertion in lifting a heavy or bulky object.[15] These injuries often do not need acute care; in contrast, the most common types of work-related injuries among youths reported in emergency room statistics are cuts and lacerations, often resulting from use of knives or other cutting instruments.[16] Table 6.7 provides a breakdown of lost workday injuries among youths for common types of injuries in 1997. In that year, sprains, strains and tears occurred more frequently during female youths' (37 percent) worktime than during that of male youths (22 percent). In contrast, cuts and lacerations were more common among male youths.

Characteristics of more severe types of injuries among youths

Table 6.6 shows that most common types of injuries are associated with relatively low median lost workdays. However, to monitor job safety among young workers it is also important to have information on the more severe work injuries, even if these injuries are relatively uncommon. For example, although lost workday injuries lasting more than 30 days were only 4.8 percent of all lost workday cases among

youths in 1997, they may entail a considerable amount of pain and suffering. Even ignoring pain and suffering, given the distribution of lost workdays by severity for 1997, the total foregone earnings of youths from lost workdays is at least 3 times greater for injuries resulting in 30 lost workdays or more than for injuries lasting a combined 1 or 2 days.[17]

The Survey of Occupational Injuries and Illnesses also provides information on the characteristics of more severe and less common injuries. Each case in the survey is coded using four different classifications: Nature of the disabling condition, the event or exposure associated with the injury, the part of the body affected, and the source directly producing the disability. Thus, the case "nurse sprains her back while lifting her patient" would be assigned four classification codes: "sprains" (for nature of disabling condition), "back" (part of body affected), "lifting" (event or exposure), and "patient" (source directly producing the disability).

The relatively small sample of cases of serious injuries among youths limits the value of examining combinations of these conditions in a given year. Analysis of pooled survey results for the years 1992 through 1997 indicates that the two combinations of event and nature of injury included at least 400 cases having median lost workdays exceeding 10 over this 6-year period. The SOII survey results indicate that there were 419 cases classified as falls from ladders that resulted in bruises and contusions; these injuries had median lost workdays of 20. There were also 460 cases classified as caught or compressed by equipment or objects that resulted in fractures; these injuries had median lost workdays of 14.

Inferences from BLS Data on the Comparative Risks to Employed Youths

There are various approaches to assessing the risks of injuries and illnesses to working youths. One ap-

Tab e 6.6. Percent distribution of cases resulting in days away from work by number of days and gender, 1992 and 1997

Days away from work	All workers		Males under age 18		Females under age 18	
	1992	1997	1992	1997	1992	1997
All cases (number)	2 331 098	1 833 380	13 447	6 678	8 517	4 478
1	15 7	16 6	18 4	18 9	22 7	17 2
2	12 9	13 0	14 1	16 2	15 1	17 9
3 to 5	20 4	20 4	24 4	31 9	30 4	35 0
6 to 10	13 6	13 1	17 4	12 0	13 9	12 7
11 to 20	11 4	11 7	10 5	11 2	8 6	8 1
21 to 30	6 4	6 7	5 9	4 4	3 8	5 2
More than 31	19 7	18 5	9 3	5 4	5 4	3 8
Median days away from work	6	5	5	4	3	4

SOURCE BLS Survey of Occupational njuries and Ilnesses

Tab e 6.7. Common types of lost work day injuries by gender, 1997

Nature of injury	Males under 18			Females under 18		
	Number	Percent	Median days	Number	Percent	Median days
Fractures	415	4 9	5	151	3 4	4
Sprains strains tears	1 902	22 3	5	1 675	37 4	4
Cuts lacerations	1 227	14 4	4	239	5 3	5
Bruises contusions	659	7 7	3	769	17 2	3
Heat burns scalds	743	8 7	5	507	11 3	5
All other natures	3 571	41 9		1 137	25 4	
Total cases	8 517	100 0	4	4 478	100 0	4

NOTE Dash indicates data not reported or data do not meet publication criteria
SOURCE BLS Survey of Occupational njuries and Ilnesses

proach would be to compare the safety of youths at work to their safety in *other* activities and locations. During their time at work, youths may be prevented from engaging in riskier activities, such as driving, and protected from risk of criminal assaults. We do not investigate this approach other than to note that, although injuries are a leading cause of death among youths, there are relatively few occupational fatalities. For example, in 1995 there were 6,622 accidental deaths from all causes (including assaults and gunshot wounds) among youths aged 15 to 19.[18] In contrast, there were 194 occupational fatalities, about 3 percent of all accidental deaths among 15- to 19-year-olds that year.

Another approach involves total counts of work injuries, but, by themselves, these do not provide much information about job risks. Additional information on the number of hours worked on the job (as a measure of the length of exposure to risk) is useful because having both types of information could allow calculation of a rate of injuries incurred per time worked. To compare injury risks of young workers with those of older workers, it is preferable to use data on total hours worked rather than employment counts because youth usually work considerably fewer hours per week and fewer weeks per year than adults. For nonfatal injuries, BLS collects data from establishments on hours worked along with information on injuries, allowing calculation of injury rates by industry, employment size, or geographic area.[19] However, the hours worked data are obtained only for the establishment's entire labor force, and thus cannot be broken down by the age of worker.

Because injury rates can not be directly calculated for young workers,

the comparisons of job risk presented in this chapter link the injury data by age to hours worked data from the Current Population Survey (CPS), a monthly survey of the U.S. labor force.[20] (See chapter 4.) CPS data indicate that using employment data to calculate injury rates overstates the relative amount of time youths are exposed to risks at work. For example, unpublished tabulations of CPS data indicate that, in 1997, 16- and 17-year-olds in the U.S. labor force worked, on average, 19.1 hours a week, less than half of the average for all workers (39.5 hours). Because the injuries that occur to youths do so with fewer hours worked on the job, comparing injuries per worker for youths to those for adults in full-time work may understate the relative risks faced by youths on the job.

The availability of hours worked data provides the possibility of measuring the *absolute* risk of employment, in the form of the expected number of injuries, or risk of a fatality, per a specified number of hours worked. Instead we follow another approach[21] in making *relative* comparisons of employment risks between youths in different jobs or industries, or with older workers in similar employment situations. This approach proposes calculation of "indexes of relative risk" that compare the risk of injury per hour worked in the particular group of workers being studied to a reference group. The formula for the index of relative risk reduces to comparing two ratios, the ratio of injuries in the study group to those in the reference group, and the respective ratio of hours worked between the two groups.[22] If the index of relative risk exceeds 1, the study group has had a disproportionate share of injuries relative to the share of hours worked in the reference group.

This report uses estimates of injuries and hours worked by two reference groups to assess occupational injury risks of youths. The two groups are: adult workers 25 to 44 years of age, and employed youths 15 to 17 years of age. We compare injuries of the youths to those of 25- to 44-year-olds because previous research has shown that occupational fatality rates increase substantially for workers older than 44; with the infirmities of age, older workers are less likely to survive work injuries.[23] Using the first reference group helps to answer the question: Are injury rates for youths lower than those for able-bodied adults in similar employment situations? Using the second reference group helps to answer the question: How do injury rates of youths vary in different employment situations?

Estimates of hours worked by youths

To compare hours worked of youths in different employment situations and with hours worked by prime-age workers, data from the CPS from 1994 to 1998 were used. Second jobs are often important in the employment of youths, such as when a youth works two part-time jobs in the summer. Since 1994, information on second jobs (such as the industry where employed) has been regularly collected in the CPS. Hours worked for various labor force groups were totaled for employment experiences over the 60 survey weeks covered by the CPS over the 5-year period 1994-98.[24]

Several characteristics of the measurement of hours worked in the CPS may limit the accuracy of comparisons of employment risks using these data. The most important limitation is that information on hours worked is collected in the CPS only for the survey week including the 12th of the month. Summing up hours worked for the year yields a total for the 12 survey weeks, whereas injuries occur every week during the year. Thus, during the month

of December, temporary work by youths over the winter school holidays is not likely to be captured in the monthly survey of labor force participation. Another significant limitation for the purpose of the employment risk comparisons is that the CPS samples only hours worked by those who are 15 years or older, whereas lost work-time injuries and occupational fatalities also occur to younger workers. The age cutoff limitation especially affects the assessment of youth fatalities in agriculture, where about one-half of the youth fatalities occurred among workers under the age of 15.

Occupational fatality risks to youths

Although the number of occupational fatalities to youths is small, a sizable proportion has occurred either in agriculture (table 6.2) or among those working in family businesses (table 6.1). The data in table 6.8 show distributions of occupational fatalities and hours worked estimates by major economic sector and class of worker for 1994 to 1998. Note that although a youth can work in different sectors of the economy over the course of the year, or hold two jobs at the same time in different sectors, the hours worked estimates from the CPS account for this variability. Panel A of table 6.8 presents these data for 15- to 17-year-old youths; panel B presents the corresponding data for adult workers aged 25 to 44 in the same employment groups. Panel A indicates that 88 percent of all worktime of youths over the 1994-98 period was spent in wage and salary jobs in private industry, compared with 6.3 percent of all work hours spent in agricultural jobs. (Youths having agricultural jobs work more hours per week than do youths in jobs outside agriculture.) The distribution of hours worked for youths is significantly different from that of the adult workers shown in panel B; adult workers spend relatively few hours in agriculture jobs and more in government jobs than do youths.

Table 6.9 uses the data displayed in table 6.8 to calculate the two in-

Tab e 6.8. **Hours worked estimates and occupational fatalities among youths and adults in agriculture, nonagriculture, and government, 1994-98**

Class and industry of worker	Occupational fatalities		Hours worked estimates[2]	
	Number	Proportion	Number	Proportion
A. Hours worked estimates and fatalities for youths, aged 15 to 17				
Private sector				
Total labor force aged 15 to 17	239	100 0	3 157 0	100 0
Agriculture				
Total	67	28 0	199 1	6 3
Wage and salary	41	17 2	134 0	4 2
Self employed and family workers	26	10 9	65 1	2 1
Nonagriculture				
Total	162	67 8	2 825 9	89 5
Wage and salary	146	61 1	2 776 9	88 0
Self employed and family workers	16	6 7	49 0	1 6
Government				
Total	10	4 2	133 0	4 2
B. Hours worked estimates and fatalities for adults, aged 25 to 44				
Private sector				
Total labor force aged 25 to 44	14 734	100 0	157 713 9	100 0
Agriculture				
Total	1 325	9 0	4 136 1	2 6
Wage and salary	758	5 1	2 360 0	1 5
Self employed and family workers	567	3 9	1 776 1	1 1
Nonagriculture				
Total	11 764	79 8	133 162 0	84 4
Wage and salary	10 338	70 2	122 656 0	77 8
Self employed and family workers	1 426	9 7	10 506 0	6 7
Government				
Total	1 645	11 1	20 415 8	12 9

Tabulations from the Census of Fatal Occupational njuries
[2] Hours worked estimates (millions of hours) are the sum of hours worked in 60 survey weeks for a subsample of Current Population Survey data that includes information on second jobs

Tab e 6.9. Indexes of relative risk of occupational fatalities among youths aged 15 to 17 and adults aged 25 to 44 by major sector and class of worker, 1994–98

Adults 25 to 44	Reference group	
	Youths 15 to 17	Adults 25 to 44
Total	1 00	0 81
Private industry		
Agriculture		
Total	4 45	1 05
Wage and salary	4 04	0 95
Self employed and family workers	5 28	1 25
Nonagriculture		
Total	0 76	0 65
Wage and salary	0 69	0 62
Self temployed and family workers	4 31	2 41
Government		
Total	0 99	0 93

SOURCE Calculated from data presented in table 6 8 with methodology adapted from John W Ruser "A Relative Risk of Analysis of Workplace Fatalities " *Compensation and Working Conditions*, January 1995

Tab e 6.10. Occupational fatalities, hours worked, and indexes of relative risk for construction by selected age group, 1994-98

Age group	Occupational fatalities	Hours worked estimates[2] (in millions)
A. Fatalities and hours worked		
Youths 15 to 17		
Levels	48	87 5
Share of total	20 1	2 8
Adults 25 to 44		
Levels	3 000	11 000
Share of total	20 4	7 0
B. Indexes of relative risk in construction [3]		
Reference group		
Youths 15 to 17 in all jobs	7 18	
Adults 25 to 44 in construction jobs	2 01	

Tabulations from the Census of Fatal Occupational njuries

[2] Hours worked estimates (millions of hours) are the sum of hours worked in 12 survey weeks for a subsample of Current Population Survey data that includes information on second jobs

[3] ndexes of relative risk adapted from John W Ruser "A Relative Risk of Analysis of Workpace Fatali ties " *Compensation and Working Conditions* January 1995

dexes of risks of an occupational fatality among youths. In the first column, the index compares the risk of a fatality per hour worked in a particular economic sector and class-of-worker status with the average risk incurred by all working youths over the 1994–98 period. For example, data in the first row of the first column shows that the risk of a fatality (per hour worked) in an agricultural wage and salary job is over 4 times as great as the average risk for all working youths. Most working time of youths is spent in relatively safe wage and salary jobs outside agriculture, hav-

ing an index of risk of only 0.69. Contributing to the higher average rate for all youths is the high risk of a fatality for youths working in family businesses, whether or not these jobs are in agriculture (with an index of 5.28) or outside agriculture (having an index of 4.31).

The second column of table 6.9 compares the fatality risk of youths' work with that of adults having the same sector and class-of-worker status. For most youths—those who have wage and salary jobs outside agriculture—the risk of a fatality is substantially less than that for adults 25 to 44

years old who are also in wage and salary jobs outside agriculture, with an index of 0.62. The average risk of an occupational fatality for youths overall is somewhat higher, but still an index of only 0.81 of the risk to adults overall. These data also indicate that the risks of a fatality to youths working in agriculture are very close to the corresponding risks to prime-age adults working in agriculture.

Not shown in table 6.9 is how the risk of an occupational fatality varies by industry outside agriculture. As table 6.10 shows, occupational fatalities in construction accounted for about one-fifth of all job-related fatalities among youths over the 1994-98 period, even though only 2.8 percent of their work hours were spent in construction employment. In part, this concentration is due to the greater risk of injury or illness for both youths and adults, as about one-fifth of all occupational fatalities among adults aged 25 to 44 also occurred in construction. Nevertheless, hours worked by youth aged 15 to 17 in the construction industry are a much smaller share of all hours worked by youths than the corresponding share is for adults. The CPS hours worked estimates indicate that the risk of an occupational fatality per hour worked was about twice as high (that is, it had an index of relative risk of 2.01) for youths as for adults working in construction in the period 1994-98.

Risk of lost worktime injuries

The scope of the BLS Survey of Occupational Injuries and Illness is limited to wage and salary workers and covers only larger agricultural employers. Consequently, risk assessments using the lost worktime injury data are restricted to comparisons among the industries in which wage and salary jobs of youths are concentrated. Table 6.11 compares the distribution of lost worktime injuries and estimates of hours worked in 1997 for youths aged 16 and 17 in the six industries employing most of them: Eating and drinking places, food stores, general merchandise stores, health

Table 6.11. **Lost worktime injuries and hours worked estimates for 16- to 17-year-olds, 1997**

Industry of worker	Lost worktime injuries			Hours worked estimates[2]	
	Number	Percent	Median work days lost	Number	Percent
Eating and drinking	3 867	46 5	4	200 0	52 8
Food stores	2 103	25 3	3	85 3	22 5
General merchandise	977	11 7	3	27 9	7 4
Health services	784	9 4	4	11 5	3 0
Amusement and recreation	412	5 0	2	42 8	11 3
Business services	173	2 1	3	11 2	3 0

Tabulations from the BLS Survey of Occupational Injuries and Illnesses
[2] Current Population Survey data for wage and salary workers only in millions of hours

services, amusement and recreation, and business services.[25] In these industries, the lost worktime injuries among 16- and 17-year-olds comprised more than three-quarters (75.9 percent) of all lost worktime injuries to youths in this age group.

Among these industries, the share of lost worktime injuries incurred in eating and drinking, food stores, and business services was roughly proportional to their representation of hours worked. However, the risk of a lost worktime injury per hour worked in health services was about 3 times that for these industries, on average. Also, the high median workdays lost in health services among youths indicate that injuries tend to be more severe than in the other industries examined here. In contrast, youths employed in amusement and recreation had, on average, only half the risk of a lost worktime injury that their counterparts in the other industries had, and the injuries tended to be less severe, as indicated by the low median of 2 lost workdays.

Anthony Barkume, a reasearch economist with the Bureau of Labor Statistics (BLS), had primary responsibility for preparation of this chapter. John Bishow, Linda Garris, Eric Sygnatur, and Mark Zak, all of BLS, prepared tabulations. John Ruser, Guy Toscano, and Janice Windau of BLS and Dawn Castillo of the National Institute for Occupational Safety and Health reviewed early drafts and provided comments and suggestions.

[1] Reviews of recent research of job safety among youths are given by National Academy of Sciences, Committee of the Health and Safety Implications of Child Labor in *Protecting Youth at Work: Health, Safety, and Development of Working Children and Adolescents in the United States* (Washington, National Academy Press, 1998); and by Dawn N. Castillo, Letitia Davis, and David Wegman, "Young Workers," in *Occupational Medicine,* July-September 1999, pp. 519-36.

[2] *Protecting Youth at Work,* p. 84.

[3] Janice Windau, Eric Sygnatur, and Guy Toscano, "Profile of work injuries incurred by young workers," *Monthly Labor Review,* June 1999, pp. 3–10.

[4] Windau, Sygnatur, and Toscano, p. 6.

[5] For more details, see chapter 2 of this report.

[6] Windau, Sygnatur, and Toscano, p. 5.

[7] Ibid., p. 6.

[8] Ibid., p. 7.

[9] Ibid., p. 7.

[10] Ibid., p. 5.

[11] Ibid., p. 9.

[12] The higher rate of growth of employment among youths since 1992 is in part due to the relatively more severe impact that the 1990-92 recession had upon job opportunities for youths.

[13] Windau, Sygnatur, and Toscano, p. 8.

[14] Changes in the age distribution of workers having lost workday injuries may have contributed to these developments.

[15] Windau, Sygnatur, and Toscano, p. 8.

[16] *Protecting Youth at Work,* p. 7.

[17] A numerical example can help to illustrate this point. Suppose total lost worktime injuries are 10,000, cases having a duration of 1 day are 18 percent of the total, cases having 2 days are 16 percent, and cases with more than 30 days are 5 percent. Then, total lost worktime associated with 1-day cases are 1,800 workdays, total lost workdays associated with 2-day cases are 3,200, but the total lost worktime associated with cases with more than 30 lost workdays would be more than 15,000. Thus, total lost worktime of the most serious cases, more than 15,000, is more than 3 times the lost worktime of the combined 1- and 2-day cases.

[18] *National Vital Statistics Report,* November 1998.

[19] These rates are published as rates per 100 full-time workers employed for a year. The methodology for their derivation is provided in *BLS Handbook of Methods,* Bulletin 2490 (Bureau of Labor Statistics, April 1997), p. 74.

[20] An extensive set of comparisons of job risk by occupation, age and nature of injury that uses CPS data is provided in chapter 3 of the *Report of the American Workforce* (U.S. Department of Labor, 1994).

[21] See John W. Ruser, " A relative risk analysis of workplace fatalities," *Compensation and Working Conditions,* January 1995, pp.18-22.

[22] *Report on the American Workforce,* 1994, p. 112.

[23] See Dawn N. Castillo and Bonita D. Malit, "Occupational injury deaths of 16- and 17-year-olds in the U.S.: trends and comparisons with older workers," *Injury Prevention,* vol. 3, 1997, pp. 277-81.

[24] In summing hours worked, the hours worked by a particular survey respondent were weighted by their sample weight. Also, to identify the characteristics of second jobs only a subsample of the CPS (the outgoing rotation group sample) was used in the calculations.

[25] See table 4.9.

Chapter 7.
The Relationship of Youth Employment to Future Educational Attainment and Labor Market Experience

Introduction

This chapter examines the relationship between youths' work activities while in school and their future educational attainment and labor market success. It begins with an overview of the economics literature concerning possible impacts. This overview is followed by an analysis of the most recent data from the National Longitudinal Survey of Youth 1979 (NLSY79). By following the lives of the NLSY79 respondents over the last 20 years, this survey permits one to describe the relationship between the number of hours and weeks of work during school months while aged 16 and 17, and later outcomes in terms of college attendance, weeks worked each year, and the number of jobs held from age 18 through 30. However, as implied by the literature review, this relationship cannot be interpreted as showing cause and effect.

The effects of youth employment

Whether youths should work during their high school years, and how much they should work, has received considerable policy attention over the last 25 years. In the mid-1970s, no fewer than three Federal Commissions studied secondary education and recommended policies to encourage youths to gain at least some work experience to ease the transition from school into adulthood.[1] In contrast, the National Commission on Excellence in Education recommended that youths spend more time on academic studies, and downplayed the value of employment during high school.[2]

The early 1990s saw a number of news media reports that generated concerns about child labor problems. Those concerns led to the 1998 study of the health, safety, and developmental impacts of youth employment by the Board on Children, Youth, and Families of the Institute of Medicine, National Research Council (NRC).[3] The NRC panel favored a new standard limiting the weekly maximum number of hours of work for 16- and 17-year-olds during the school year.

Over this same period, numerous economic research studies have examined the issue of the long-run effects of working while young. In general, researchers, even when finding positive effects, are deliberately cautious in interpreting their results. Using data from the NLSY79 survey, V. Joseph Hotz and others find that men who worked while in high school have higher average hourly wages at age 27 ($10.75) than those who did not ($9.69).[4] As the authors point out, however, it is possible that these results do not demonstrate that working while in school has positive impacts.[5] Instead, the findings may simply reflect pre-existing differences among groups of youths — that is, more able or "better connected" youths acquire jobs during their early years, and these same youths have better subsequent employment and schooling opportunities.

Echoing this same caution, the 1998 NRC report states: "Young people who work may be different before they begin to work than those who do not work and those who work long hours may be different than those who work

fewer hours. For example, adolescents who are not interested in school may choose to work longer hours than those who enjoy school...."[6] Another reason for caution is that many studies have been able to observe only early outcomes from working while young, leaving open the question of whether effects lessen with age.[7] Yet another consideration is that how many hours one works while young may be critically related to later outcomes, which is not always addressed in studies.

What does the research show? The 1998 NRC report reviewed the available research and concluded that: "Low intensity employment may support post-secondary educational outcomes while high-intensity employment may hinder them."[8] In general, although studies differ in their samples and definitions, they often use 20 or fewer hours of work per week as the dividing line between high- and low-intensity work.

As noted, there has been some question about whether the positive effects found in studies are temporary, and will dissipate or disappear at older ages. A recent study by Audrey Light examined the effect of high school employment on wages throughout the 9 years following high school for men who did not continue their education.[9] Her research, which allows for different intensities of work, used the NLSY79. She found that high school employment has a positive, skill-enhancing effect on wages for the first 6 years after graduation, which disappears by 9 years after graduation.

These results contrast with those of Christopher Ruhm, who also used the NLSY79 but concluded that working during the senior year in high school is associated with positive labor market outcomes 6 to 9 years later, with particularly large benefits associated with moderate work hours for female youths.[10] The positive outcomes include higher annual earnings, a greater likelihood of receiving fringe benefits, and having higher status occupations. Ruhm, however, also finds a negative impact of working while young on the amount of education received, and that work during the sophomore and junior years of high school is not associated with positive future labor market outcomes.

Finally, the recent study by Hotz and others, which also used the NLSY79 data but for young men only, concludes that findings of generally positive impacts may be sensitive to the choice of method used for the analysis. The authors' preferred method provides estimates that imply that going to school and not working has much bigger payoffs to wages at age 27 than combining school and part-time work.[11] One drawback to this study, however, is that it does not examine the impact on adult wages of the number of hours of work each week (for example, fewer than or more than 20 hours per week) or the timing of work (such as during the

school year or the summer) while young.

In conclusion, the evidence on the impact of working while young is somewhat mixed. These studies generally point to a positive impact on the likelihood of being employed, but do not find a lasting effect in the form of receiving higher wages. There also are important caveats to consider, such as possible systematic differences, not fully accounted for in the research studies, in the characteristics of those who choose to work while young—especially those who work more hours, as compared to those who do not work or who work fewer hours. And there is still the question of whether positive effects that are found are temporary and will dissipate or disappear at older ages.

Evidence from the NLSY79

This part of the chapter describes labor market experience in young adulthood and educational attainment separately for individuals who differ on the basis of their work activities while in school. The data used are from the NLSY79, a nationally representative sample of 12,686 young men and women who were born between January 1, 1957 and December 31, 1964. The first NLSY79 interview took place in 1979, when respondents were aged 14 to 22. Respondents were interviewed annually through 1994 and are now surveyed biennially. This analysis uses data for respondents in the birth years 1962-64, for whom details on employment are available beginning at age 16.

These individuals are now in their thirties, and thus the NLSY79 can be used to examine the relationship between youth employment and later educational and employment experience. Without controlling for other factors that can influence outcomes—in particular, the characteristics of those who choose to work (and those who choose to work more intensively) during high school—the tables and charts shown below cannot imply a causality between youth employment and longer-term outcomes. However, given the unique

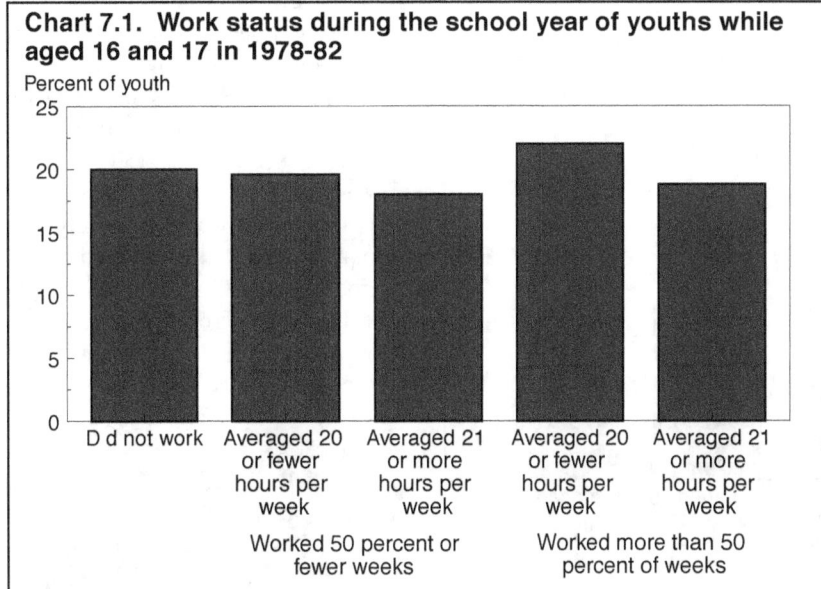

Chart 7.1. Work status during the school year of youths while aged 16 and 17 in 1978-82

Percent of youth

Chart 7.2. Work status during the school year of youths while aged 16 and 17 in 1978-82, by sex

Percent of youth

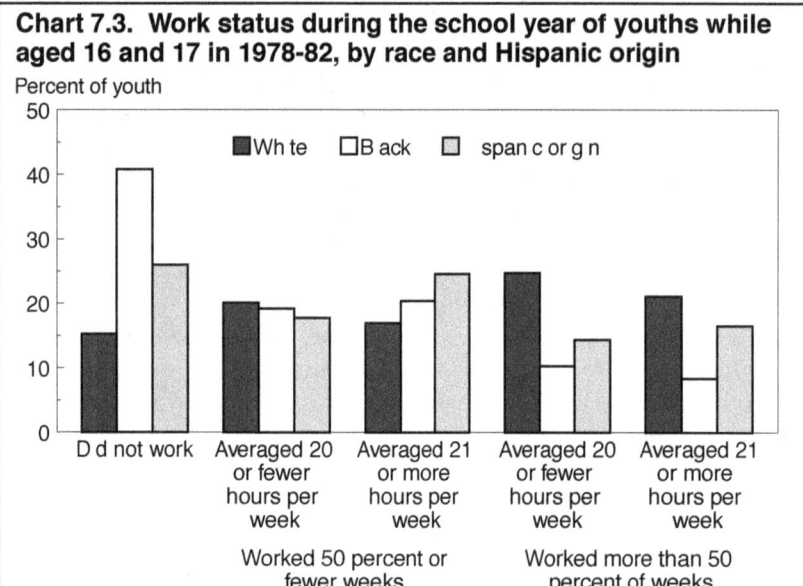

Chart 7.3. Work status during the school year of youths while aged 16 and 17 in 1978-82, by race and Hispanic origin

Percent of youth

Legend: ■ White □ Black ▨ Hispanic origin

Categories: Did not work | Averaged 20 or fewer hours per week / Averaged 21 or more hours per week (Worked 50 percent or fewer weeks) | Averaged 20 or fewer hours per week / Averaged 21 or more hours per week (Worked more than 50 percent of weeks)

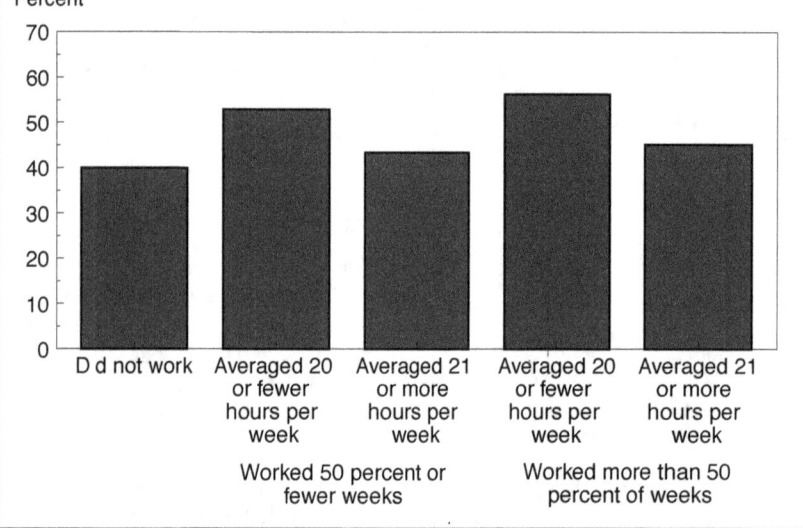

Chart 7.4. Percent of individuals with at least some college education at age 30, by average hours worked during school weeks while aged 16 and 17 in 1978-82

Percent

Categories: Did not work | Averaged 20 or fewer hours per week / Averaged 21 or more hours per week (Worked 50 percent or fewer weeks) | Averaged 20 or fewer hours per week / Averaged 21 or more hours per week (Worked more than 50 percent of weeks)

longitudinal nature of the data, they provide valuable insight into the possible relationship between youth employment and adult outcomes.

School-year employment while aged 16 and 17

The findings in this section pertain to work experience during the school year while aged 16 and 17. Note that work experience while 16 and 17 for this group born in 1962-64 occurred during calendar years 1978-82. These years include the last 2 years of a business cycle expansion and both the 1980 and 1981-82 recessions.

To highlight the separate effects of the number of weeks worked and the number of hours worked during the week, individuals are grouped into five categories of work intensity throughout this analysis and in the sections that follow. They are:

(1) youths who did not work during school weeks while 16 and 17;

(2) youths who worked 50 percent of school weeks or fewer, and averaged 20 or fewer hours of work per week;

(3) youths who worked 50 percent of school weeks or fewer, and

averaged more than 20 hours of work per week;

(4) youths who worked more than 50 percent of school weeks, and averaged 20 or fewer hours of work per week; and

(5) youths who worked more than 50 percent of school weeks, and averaged more than 20 hours of work per week.

Twenty percent of these individuals never worked at any point during the school year while they were aged 16 and 17.[12] (See chart 7.1.) About 41 percent worked more than half of all school weeks. These youths are fairly evenly split between averaging 20 or fewer hours per week and more than 20 hours per week.[13] The same is true for those who worked a relatively low percentage of school weeks (50 percent or fewer).

Male youths were more likely than female youths to have worked during school weeks (83 and 78 percent, respectively). (See chart 7.2.) In addition, working male youths averaged more hours of work per school week than did working female youths.

Black 16- and 17-year-olds were substantially less likely to have worked during school weeks (59 percent) than were whites (85 percent) or Hispanics (74 percent). (See chart 7.3.) Hispanics were more likely to work high average hours and a relatively low percentage of weeks, as compared to whites and blacks. Whites, on the other hand, were more likely to average high numbers of hours per week and to work a relatively high percentage of weeks compared to blacks and Hispanics.

There also were significant differences in the likelihood of working based on family income. Youths in families with incomes of less than $25,000 were less likely to work than were youths in families in higher income groups. (See table 7.1.) Youths in families with incomes over $70,000 were both more likely to average low hours per week and to work a high percentage of school weeks, compared with youths in lower family income groups.

In summary, a majority of 16- and 17-year-old youths in 1978-82 worked at some point during the school term and, as is the case for today's youths, their work patterns varied notably by demographic characteristics. For example, in chapter 3, we saw that male youths aged 14 and 15 in 1994-97 were more likely than female youths to work a relatively high percentage of school weeks and to average high numbers of hours during those weeks.[14] The same pattern is found for 16- and 17-year-olds in 1978-82. Whites in both cohorts are also more likely than blacks or Hispanics to work a high percentage of school weeks and to average high hours during those weeks. We next examine the relationship between youth employment while aged 16 and 17 and later educational and employment experience.

Educational attainment at age 30

Consistent with the general findings in the literature, individuals who worked but averaged 20 hours or fewer per school week while aged 16 and 17 were more likely than other youths to have at least some college education by age 30. (See chart 7.4.) More specifically, more than half of youths who worked 20 or fewer hours per week while in school had at least some college education by age 30. In contrast, fewer than half of those who did not work or who worked more than 20 hours a week had achieved similar education levels by age 30. These findings hold regardless of whether one worked more or fewer than 50 percent of weeks while in school. The same pattern also is generally evident for men and women separately. (See chart 7.5.)

The overall findings just discussed hold for whites as well. In contrast, educational attainment of blacks and Hispanics is not so clearly related to hours worked while aged 16 and 17. Fewer than half of blacks in each of the five work intensity groups had any college education by age 30. Well over half of Hispanics who worked more than 50 percent of school weeks but 20 or fewer hours a week had some college education by age 30, whereas fewer than half of Hispanics in each of the other work intensity categories had any college education. (See chart 7.6.)

Work experience while aged 18 through 30

The NLSY79 provides detailed work history information. This analysis examines the percent of weeks worked by individuals over the years when they are aged 18 to 30. The analysis continues to focus on groups divided by work intensity while aged 16 and 17 and in school.

In general, what emerges is that each step up in the percent of school weeks spent in work is associated with a step up in the percent of weeks worked in the following 13 years, regardless of the category of hours worked per week. (See chart 7.7.) In particular, individuals who did not work during school weeks while aged 16 and 17 worked 64 percent of weeks from age 18 through 30. Those who worked 50 percent of

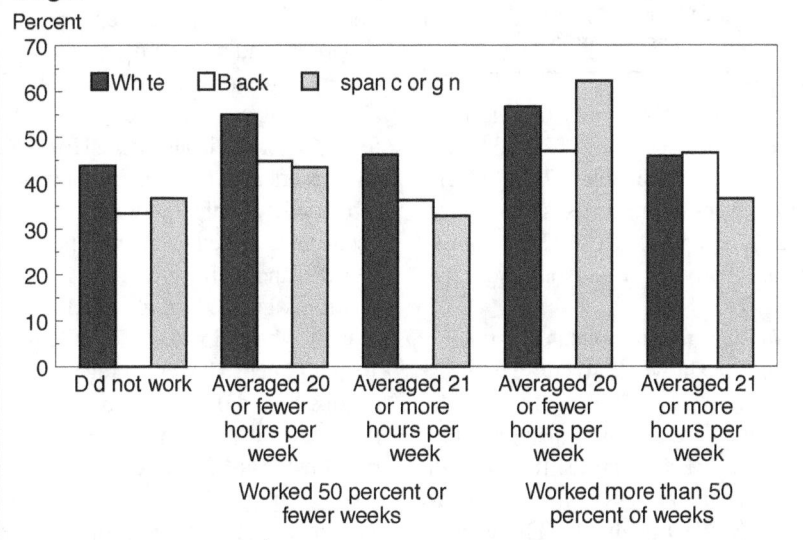

Chart 7.5. Percent of individuals with at least some college education at age 30, by average hours worked during school weeks while aged 16 and 17 in 1978-82, by sex

Chart 7.6. Percent of individuals with at least some college education at age 30, by average hours worked during school weeks while aged 16 and 17 in 1978-82, by race and Hispanic origin

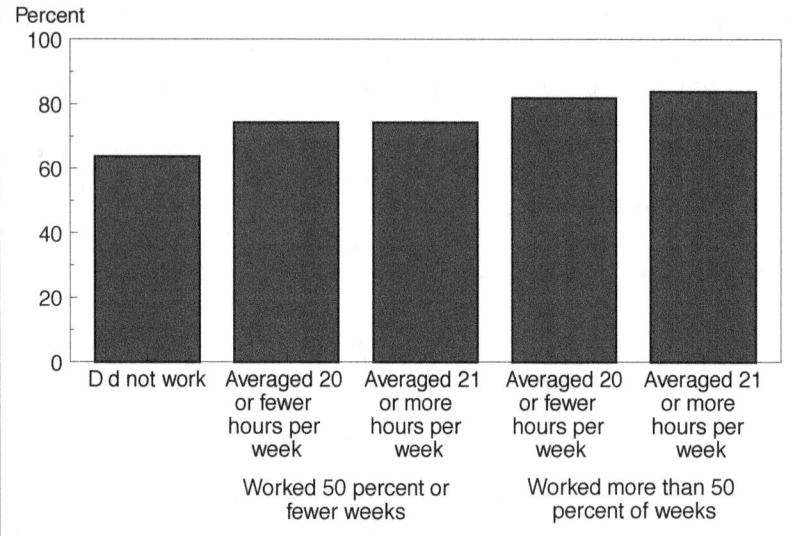

Chart 7.7. Percent of weeks worked while aged 18 to 30 in 1980-95, by average hours worked during school weeks while aged 16 and 17 in 1978-82

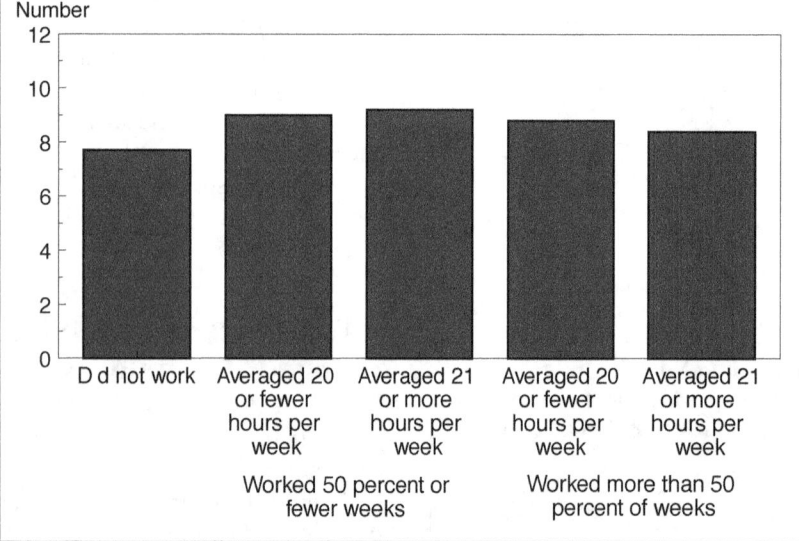

Chart 7.8. Average number of jobs held by individuals while aged 18 to 30 in 1980-95, by average hours worked during school weeks while aged 16 and 17 in 1978-82

school weeks or less while aged 16 and 17 worked an average of 74 percent of weeks while aged 18 to 30. The percentage is even higher (between 82 and 84 percent, depending on the category of hours worked per week) for youths who worked more than 50 percent of school weeks at these ages. This overall step-up pattern also holds over age 18 to 30 for both men and women and regardless of race and ethnicity.

This pattern—each step up in school workweeks while 16 and 17 is associated with a step up in workweeks

when older—also holds for the narrower age ranges of 18 to 22, 23 to 26, and 27 to 30. (See table 7.2.) The percent of weeks worked rises from ages 18 to 22 to ages 23 to 26, but then remains steady while persons are aged 27 to 30.

Various measures in this report have generally shown that white youths work more than black youths. Table 7.2 indicates that whites also typically work more weeks from age 18 to 30 than do blacks, regardless of their work intensity while in school. The excep-

tion is that, for individuals with the most intensive work experience while young (worked more than 50 percent of school weeks and averaged 21 or more hours per week), there is no significant difference between the percent of weeks worked by blacks and that worked by whites from age 18 through 30.

Table 7.2 shows that, from age 23 through 30, those with some college work more weeks than do those with no college. For those 18 through 22, however, this reverses, probably because individuals in the higher education category engage in further education during those years. The overall step-up pattern in workweeks for young adults associated with their school workweeks while aged 16 and 17 holds for individuals in both the higher and lower educational groups. For those individuals with some college, however, the percent of weeks worked while aged 27 to 30 differs little among those with different work experiences while young.

Number of jobs held while aged 18 through 30

This section examines the number of jobs individuals held during various periods when they were aged 18 through 30, again grouping them by hours and percent of weeks worked during school weeks while they were aged 16 and 17. Young workers have a great deal of job mobility during their early years in the labor market, and thus hold a relatively high number of jobs. Early job mobility may represent job shopping, and may be beneficial for a variety of reasons. For example, it can allow young workers to learn about different work environments. However, as workers age, they tend to have less job mobility, which may represent the occurrence of better matches between workers and their jobs.[15]

From age 18 through age 30, individuals who did not work while aged 16 and 17 held a lower average number of jobs than did those who worked at these ages. (See chart 7.8.) While this relationship also holds for the narrower range from age 18 to 22, across the older age ranges the number of jobs is fairly similar across all categories of work while young. (See table 7.3.)

Men held an average of 8.9 jobs and women held an average of 8.4 jobs from age 18 to age 30. While aged 18 to 22, men and women held about the same number of jobs within all categories of work while 16 and 17. From age 27 to age 30, however, men held a higher number of jobs than did women within most categories of work while 16 and 17.

Whites held more jobs (8.7) than did blacks or Hispanics (8.3 and 8.2 respectively) from age 18 through age 30. Whites tend to hold more jobs from age 18 to 22 than do blacks across most work categories while young. However, from age 27 to 30, whites hold either the same number or fewer jobs than do blacks within each category of work while young.

Individuals with at least some college education held 9.1 jobs from age 18 through 30, in contrast to 8.2 jobs held by those with a high school diploma or less education. Over these ages, within both education categories, individuals who did not work while 16 and 17 generally held a lower average number of jobs than did those who worked while 16 and 17.

Conclusion

In summary, 80 percent of individuals born in the years 1962 to 1964 worked at some point during the school year when they were aged 16 and 17. Individuals who worked while aged 16 and 17 but spent 20 or fewer hours per week at work were more likely than others to have acquired some college education by age 30. In addition, a higher percentage of weeks worked while young is associated with greater work experience through age 30. This does not necessarily imply that early work experience causes these later outcomes. For example, it may be that those who work while young are also those with higher motivation or more economic opportunities. Thus, although those with work experience while young have certain desirable outcomes, these outcomes may in fact be due to the underlying characteristics of the youths themselves.

This chapter was contributed by Donna Rothstein, a research economist with the Bureau of Labor Statistics, and Marilyn Manser, an associate commissioner with the Bureau. The authors thank Michael Horrigan for helpful comments, and Alexander Eidelman for excellent research assistance.

[1] See the National Commission on the Reform of Secondary Education, *The Reform of Secondary Education* (New York, McGraw Hill, 1973); the President's Science Advisory Committee, *Youth: Transition to Adulthood* (Chicago, The University of Chicago Press, 1974); and the National Panel on High School and Adolescent Education, *The Education of Adolescents: The Final Report and Recommendations of the National Panel on High School and Adolescent Education* (Washington, U.S. Department of Health, Education, and Welfare, Office of Education, 1976).

[2] See National Commission on Excellence in Education, *A Nation at Risk: The Imperative for Education Reform* (Washington, U.S. Government Printing Office, 1983).

[3] See National Research Council, *Protecting Youth at Work* (Washington, National Academy Press, 1998). The NRC study was sponsored by the National Institute for Occupational Safety and Health with support by other agencies, including the Wage and Hour Division of the U.S. Department of Labor. The study also provided a number of recommendations for possible changes to regulations and data collection and for increased research.

[4] V. Joseph Hotz, Lixin Xu, Marta Tienda, and Avner Ahituv, "Are There Returns to the Wages of Young Men from Working While in School," Unpublished paper (University of California at Los Angeles, Department of Economics, June 1999).

[5] Hotz and others, "Are There Returns," p. 14.

[6] Technically, these estimation problems arise because of the existence of selection effects and unobserved heterogeneity. See National Research Council, *Protecting Youth at Work*, p. 113.

[7] See the National Research Council, *Protecting Youth at Work*, pp. 121-24, for a more detailed summary and references to the earlier literature.

[8] National Research Council, *Protecting Youth at Work*, p. 117.

[9] See Audrey Light, "High School Employment, High School Curriculum, and Post-school Wages," *Economics of Education Review*, vol. 18, 1999, 291-309.

[10] See Christopher J. Ruhm, "Is High School Employment Consumption or Investment?" *Journal of Labor Economics*, vol. 15, no. 4, 1997, pp. 735-76.

[11] Their preferred econometric technique (the "dynamic selection control" estimation technique) controls for the impact of unobserved differences between respondents that affect their decisions to work while enrolled in school, and also influence the wage offers they receive at older ages.

[12] The expression "while 16 and 17" refers to the 2-year period between the youths' 16th and 18th birthdays. School weeks exclude those in June, July, August, the last week in December, and the first week in January.

If a youth dropped out or graduated from high school while 17, only those school weeks prior to this occurrence are used in calculations. Youths who dropped out or graduated from high school while 16 are excluded.

[13] Hours are averaged over school weeks in which the youth worked. Hours are defined according to the following methodology: Survey respondents report usual hours per week as of each job's stop date (or the interview date for ongoing jobs). Hours reported for each job are then back-filled to the job's start date. Therefore, there is a total number of hours worked across all jobs reported for each week a youth worked. Hours per week are then averaged over the academic weeks worked while age 16 and 17 (prior to dropping out or graduating from school). Given this methodology, work hours from other time periods (for example, summer, after the youth turned 18, after the youth dropped out or graduated from school) are sometimes back-filled into school-year weeks. This can potentially lead to an overstatement of average hours. On average, about one-third (32 percent) of academic weeks worked while 16 and 17 were back-filled with hours from another time period—8 percent of school year weeks worked were back-filled with summer hours, 15 percent were back-filled with work hours information from after the youth turned 18, and 9 percent were back-filled with work hours information from other time periods, such as subsequent to dropping out or graduating from school.

[14] In chapter 3, "high" hours are defined as 15 or more, rather than 21 or more as in this chapter. We chose a different hours break-point because we examined work behavior of younger youths in chapter 3 (14- and 15-year-olds), who, on average, work fewer hours during the school-term.

[15] For additional discussion, see *Work and Family: Jobs Held and Weeks Worked by Young Adults*, Report 827, August 1992, Bureau of Labor Statistics.

Table 7.1. **Work status during the school year of youths aged 16 to 17 in 1978-82: Individuals aged 14 to 16 on December 31, 1978, by sex, race, Hispanic origin, and family income**

Age in 1978-82 and characteristic	Did not work	Worked 50 percent or fewer of school weeks		Worked more than 50 percent of school weeks	
		Averaged 20 or fewer hours per week	Averaged 21 or more hours per week	Averaged 20 or fewer hours per week	Averaged 21 or more hours per week
Total, aged 16 and 17 in 1978-82..............	20.0	19.6	18.0	22.0	18.8
Male youths	17.5	17.9	20.3	20.7	21.7
Female youths	22.5	21.3	15.6	23.4	15.9
White	15.3	20.1	17.0	24.8	21.1
Black	40.8	19.2	20.4	10.3	8.4
Hispanic origin	26.0	17.8	24.6	14.4	16.5
Family income in 1979 (in 1996 dollars) ...					
Less than $25,000	31.6	18.8	22.3	12.4	13.7
$25,000 to 44,999	23.6	19.3	17.0	19.7	18.8
$45,000 to 69,999	11.2	22.3	16.8	24.7	23.4
$70,000 and over.................................	11.4	21.2	14.8	33.8	17.9

NOTE: The National Longitudinal Survey of Youth 1979 consists of persons aged 14 to 22 in 1979. The columns exclude individuals who had turned 16 before 1978.

Rows do not add to 100 due to the nonreporting of information on hours and weeks of work for a small number of working respondents.

Race and Hispanic origin groups are mutually exclusive. Totals include American Indians, Alaskan Natives, and Asians and Pacific Islanders, not shown separately.

Table 7.2. **Percent of weeks employed for individuals aged 18 to 30 in 1980-95, categorized by percent of school weeks and number of hours worked while aged 16 and 17, by age, education, sex, race, and Hispanic origin**

Age in 1980-95 and characteristic	Total	Did not work	Worked 50 percent or fewer of school weeks		Worked more than 50 percent of school weeks	
			Averaged 20 or fewer hours per week	Averaged 21 or more hours per week	Averaged 20 or fewer hours per week	Averaged 21 or more hours per week
Total, aged 18 to 30 in 1980-95	75.7	63.8	74.3	74.3	81.8	83.9
Men	81.3	70.1	79.6	78.1	87.1	89.0
Women	70.0	58.7	69.8	69.2	77.0	76.6
White	78.1	67.7	75.7	76.5	82.5	83.9
Black	64.6	56.2	66.7	68.0	72.1	82.5
Hispanic origin	72.7	62.7	72.9	70.7	79.9	84.8
High school or less	73.3	59.5	71.8	72.0	82.5	83.0
Some college or more	78.3	70.0	76.6	77.3	81.2	85.0
Total, aged 18 to 22 in 1980-87	65.9	48.0	63.5	63.0	75.5	78.8
Men	69.2	52.8	64.6	65.0	76.7	83.0
Women	62.5	44.1	62.5	60.2	74.5	73.1
White	68.9	52.0	65.6	64.7	76.6	78.8
Black	51.3	40.0	51.4	58.9	60.3	75.7
Hispanic origin	62.8	47.9	63.5	58.6	74.4	82.0
High school or less	67.4	48.4	65.3	65.2	80.7	81.2
Some college or more	64.2	47.2	61.9	60.1	71.5	76.0
Total, aged 23 to 26 in 1985-91	80.5	70.5	79.8	80.1	85.0	87.1
Men	86.5	78.0	85.7	84.0	90.3	92.8
Women	74.5	64.6	74.8	74.9	80.4	79.3
White	82.8	74.7	81.1	82.4	85.7	87.2
Black	70.6	62.2	74.6	74.2	77.1	85.9
Hispanic origin	76.5	69.1	74.2	76.7	79.9	87.5
High school or less	76.2	64.4	75.3	75.9	82.8	84.8
Some college or more	85.2	79.8	83.7	85.6	86.7	89.9
Total, aged 27 to 30 in 1989-95	80.8	73.2	79.7	80.1	85.0	85.8
Men	88.2	80.4	88.7	85.3	93.5	91.5
Women	73.4	67.6	72.0	73.1	77.3	77.8
White	82.8	76.8	80.7	82.7	85.5	86.0
Black	71.7	66.2	74.1	71.0	78.2	86.2
Hispanic origin	78.2	71.7	79.8	76.7	82.5	84.8
High school or less	76.4	66.3	74.8	75.1	83.7	83.5
Some college or more	85.7	83.4	84.0	86.8	85.9	88.7

NOTE: The National Longitudinal Survey of Youth 1979 consists of persons aged 14 to 22 in 1979. The columns exclude individuals who had turned 16 before 1978.

Race and Hispanic origin groups are mutually exclusive. Totals include American Indians, Alaskan Natives, and Asians and Pacific Islanders, not shown separately.

Tab e 7.3. **Number of jobs held by individuals aged 18 to 30 in 1980-95, categorized by percent of school weeks and number of hours worked while aged 16 and 17, by age, education, sex, race, and Hispanic origin**

Age n 1980-95 and character st c	Tota	D d not work	Worked 50 percent or fewer of schoo weeks		Worked more than 50 percent of schoo weeks	
			Averaged 20 or fewer hours per week	Averaged 21 or more hours per week	Averaged 20 or fewer hours per week	Averaged 21 or more hours per week
Tota , aged 18 to 30 n 1980-95	8.6	7.7	9.0	9.2	8.8	8.4
Men	8.9	8.3	9.3	9.3	8.8	8.8
Women	8.4	7.2	8.8	9.1	8.8	7.9
Wh te	8.7	8.1	9.1	9.3	8.7	8.4
B ack	8.3	7.4	8.5	9.3	8.7	9.0
H span c or g n	8.2	6.2	9.5	8.4	9.5	8.6
H gh schoo or ess	8.2	7.1	8.9	9.2	8.0	8.1
Some co ege or more	9.1	8.5	9.1	9.3	9.5	8.9
Tota , aged 18 to 22 n 1980-87	4.5	3.5	4.7	4.7	4.9	4.6
Men	4.5	3.7	4.7	4.7	4.9	4.6
Women	4.4	3.4	4.7	4.7	5.0	4.5
Wh te	4.6	3.9	4.8	4.8	5.0	4.6
B ack	3.7	3.0	4.1	4.4	4.3	4.2
H span c or g n	4.2	2.8	5.0	4.3	5.0	4.5
H gh schoo or ess	4.1	3.2	4.4	4.6	4.5	4.3
Some co ege or more	4.8	4.0	4.9	4.8	5.3	5.0
Tota , aged 23 to 26 n 1985-91	3.0	2.8	3.0	3.0	3.1	3.0
Men	3.1	3.1	3.0	3.0	3.0	3.2
Women	2.8	2.5	3.0	3.0	3.1	2.6
Wh te	3.0	2.9	3.0	3.0	3.1	2.9
B ack	2.9	2.7	3.0	3.1	2.8	3.2
H span c or g n	2.8	2.4	3.0	2.7	3.1	3.0
H gh schoo or ess	2.7	2.5	2.9	2.9	2.7	2.8
Some co ege or more	3.2	3.2	3.2	3.1	3.3	3.2
Tota , aged 27 to 30 n 1989-95	3.0	3.0	3.1	3.3	2.8	2.9
Men	3.2	3.2	3.3	3.4	2.9	3.2
Women	2.8	2.8	2.9	3.2	2.7	2.6
Wh te	3.0	3.0	3.1	3.3	2.7	2.9
B ack	3.2	3.0	3.0	3.4	3.2	3.5
H span c or g n	2.9	2.4	3.1	3.0	3.2	3.0
H gh schoo or ess	3.0	2.8	3.3	3.4	2.7	3.0
Some co ege or more	3.0	3.1	2.9	3.3	2.9	2.9

NOTE: The Nat ona Long tud na Survey of Youth 1979 cons sts of persons aged 14 to 22 n 1979. The co umns exc ude nd v dua s who had turned 16 before 1978.

Race and H span c or g n groups are mutua y exc us ve. Tota s nc ude Amer can Ind ans, A askan Nat ves, and As ans and Pac f c Is anders, not shown separate y.